We would like to acknowledge all the people we have worked with, too numerous to mention, who have contributed to the writing of this book.

Contents

Introduction

Active Learning: A Trainer's Guide is a book for trainers: by which we mean that it is for people whose work is to enable the professional development of others. We are aware that nowadays this includes a broad constituency; more and more people are becoming trainers, or are adding the role of trainer to their other work-roles. Training is a growth industry in every sense of the word!

We are aware also that there are many different kinds of trainer, working in or for many different professional groupings. There are in-house trainers working exclusively for one organisation or department. There are external trainers who apply their expertise to the specific demands of a variety of clients. There are trainers who work nationally for people from one or several professions. There are trainers who are based at training centres, offering particular kinds of experience to one or several professions or cross-professional groups. And so on.

This book is for *all* trainers, whatever situation they work in, whichever professional groupings they work for, whether they are full-time or occasional, experienced or inexperienced. It is for anyone who is involved in the business of enabling people to become competent — or more competent — in skills that are integral to their work, or the work that they aspire to.

Active Learning: A Trainer's Guide is a resource for trainers who are concerned with their own professional development. It will be of interest to anybody involved in teaching, training, or education, either as a practitioner or a learner. But the book will be of more direct benefit to you if you are a practising trainer, and if you are committed to the notion that trainers need to care for their own development as well as the development of others.

This book is about our experiences as trainers and the lessons we have learned. It gives you the opportunity to:

- share the experience of two trainers who have worked extensively in a range of training contexts;
- explore the principles and processes involved in enabling adults to learn actively and effectively;
- consider the strategies that we have developed for dealing with problems that commonly arise in training situations;
- review your current practice and, perhaps, identify some different approaches, strategies and techniques that you can apply in your work.

Trainers and professional development

Neither of us planned to become trainers. Jill was the leader at a teacher's centre in Blackburn. She worked with groups of teachers on aspects of curriculum development. She was not an expert. Her role was to facilitate, to help groups of teachers grapple with the changes they were facing in their jobs. Hank was a community worker, working with groups of local people in Oldham to enable them to take more control of their living environments, to develop the skills to negotiate with local authorities and to work together towards common goals. From those experiences of working with groups, we began to develop the skills and interests that led us to become trainers. Training became the way of working that gave us the greatest satisfaction.

Both of us have worked principally as 'external' trainers. We have been brought in by organisations who have wanted to use our expertise to assist in their programmes for staff development. In Jill's case, this has been mainly with local education authorities, training their teaching and advisory staff. Hank has worked for a wide range of organisations in the public and voluntary sector, training different professional groupings: recreation managers, police, social workers, health workers, youth and play workers, Intermediate Treatment and Probation Office staff. Recently, Jill retired from her position as national director of the Active Tutorial Work Project, which trained teachers throughout the UK in the techniques and philosophy of active, student-centred learning. Hank has recently taken up a post with the management development division of a leading training consultancy working in the private sector.

Most of the trainers we know have become trainers through a similar combination of accident, design, and demand. In general, it seems that there are two routes into the training industry. There are people who have always had an interest or involvement in learning and personal development. Their previous work may have been related to training in some way — as a teacher, or personnel officer, or group-worker. They have been personally motivated to extend existing skills so that they are applicable in the training context.

Others have come into training from their experience of the subject matter that they are training in. They may have been doing a job for several years, and then transferred into a training department to pass on their knowledge and experience to others. In many cases, they haven't been personally motivated to become trainers. Training is an attractive, sometimes the only, option for extending their careers.

In both of these cases, it is unusual for people to receive in-depth training in order to develop their training skills. More often than not it is assumed that people will make effective trainers because of their interests, skills, experience and personality. This is often true. It is also true that, once in post, there is little opportunity for people to evaluate and develop their skills, or to explore alternative approaches to the promotion of learning. This is not just because they don't have the time. Access to 'trainer training' is not readily available. The only source of learning available to most trainers is their own experience.

Learning whilst enabling the learning of others, however, is not easy. It requires discipline and a capacity for reflection and honest self-appraisal. Most of all it requires time — time to reflect on experience, to appraise effectiveness, and to explore other possibilities. Time is rarely available.

We have written this book because we are aware of how important it has been for us as trainers to be continually developing. We know, too, of how few opportunities exist which can contribute to that development. This was highlighted for us when we first started to discuss the possibility of writing together. As we compared experiences, we became aware of how many of those experiences were common to both of us. There was great relief in realising this commonality, in identifying the generic qualities of the training scenario. And as we shared the different ways we have of managing group learning, of motivating others, of dealing with problems, we were reminded of how lonely the trainer can become, how hard it can be to admit that there are difficulties, to be open to the possibility that there are other ways of doing things. It is a loneliness that we had long since taken for granted. The continual expectation from the learning group that the trainer is authoritative and competent is a pressure that works against open self-assessment. As we talked, we became excited by the rare opportunity to share our uncertainty and vulnerability.

Philosophies of learning and training

We believe absolutely that there is no one way to train. We found, in talking together, that the different contexts in which we worked resulted inevitably in different approaches, different techniques and strategies. It was that difference that was so exciting for both of us initially, and confirmed our belief that rigid adherence to one way of working is dangerous, and can lead to a dogmatic disregard of the learner and their individual needs.

Implicit in that acceptance of difference is a philosophy that we both share, and which underpins this book: that for learning to be effective, the learner must be actively engaged in and in control of their own learning. We call this Active Learning, but it is called many other things by people who share that basic philosophy, and who are concerned to shift the locus of power in the training scenario away from the trainer and towards the learner.

For us, active learning can be summarised by the following principles. It is a process which:

- actively involves the learner in their own learning;
- starts the learning process from the needs, desires and perceptions of the learner;
- structures the learning experience so that it supports the learner in clarifying and expressing their needs;
- creates an environment conducive to learner-centred learning;
- believes that the primary responsibility for and control over learning should be shared with the learner;
- perceives the role of the trainer as that of enabler and facilitator of learning;
- assumes that everyone in the learning group has a positive contribution to make, based on their experience, knowledge, and talents;
- assumes that the trainer has as much to learn from the learners as they have from the trainer and from each other;
- promotes the independence of the learner;

- structures the learning process so that it is intrinsically developmental;
- perceives self-evaluation as a primary learning tool, and recognises that the most useful assessment for a learner is self-assessment;
- perceives any necessary external assessment as the product of negotiation between the trainer and the learner.

The general philosophy which governs these principles is, it seems to us, becoming increasingly accepted in the training world. The principles may vary according to different ways of working. But the philosophy of empowering the learner through active engagement of their involvement and responsibility is becoming the dominant training philosophy. A group of trainers from a large organisation that Hank has worked with referred to the end of 'chalk and talk' and its replacement by the 'facilitation method' as their new strategy for training. The labels were different but the ideas were the same. The movement away from traditional, teacher-centred methods towards more active, participative and experiential learning methods is gathering momentum in the sphere of adult learning. There are signs that it is also gathering momentum in the sphere of secondary education.

For many people this shift in methodology represents a political or philosophical movement. Within the politics of education it is an extremely significant shift, not least because it is recognised that such methods lead to more effective learning. Effectiveness is measured in the short term by the degree to which the learner can use what they have learnt to improve their work performance. But more significantly, it is measured in the long term by other criteria — the capacity to create within the learner the inner resources with which to manage their own continuing development.

In active learning, the learner moves to centre stage, no longer a recipient of, but a participant in, the learning process. The process becomes dependent on the individual contributions of the learning group, and therefore focuses on and is concerned with their individuality. There is perceived to be a holistic connection between professional development and personal growth, and so the outcomes of the learning process embrace both dimensions: the personal and the professional.

The integration of the professional and the personal in active learning is not always overt or immediate. We know that if we advertised our courses with reference to personal development, people would shy away from them. Working people generally perceive their training needs in terms of professional development, by which they mean the acquisition or development of skills of practical relevance to their work. But skills, apart from the purely mechanical, aren't learnt in a vacuum. Skills are instrumental ways of doing or being. The values placed on any skill are representative of a set of attitudes which may or may not be consistent with the attitudes of the individual learner. The exploration of this consistency can lead to a heightened self-awareness which is applicable in both the professional and personal aspects of the learner's life.

All training, therefore, has the potential to contribute to a developmental continuum:

skills -------------------- > attitudes -------------------- > self-awareness

and the trainer can select how far they want to go along that continuum, either as a general rule, or in specific instances. We are aware that for many trainers the integration of the personal and the professional may seem irrelevant to the reality of their work. An overt concern with personal development may be inappropriate, even irresponsible. The primary need for skill development within the professional context may not allow for exploration of implications within the personal domain. Other trainers may feel that the achievement of professional goals is undermined by the preclusion of personal issues. Whatever the trainer's objective, however, we believe that any training event has the potential to contribute to a learner's personal development. For ourselves, we are both committed to going as far along the developmental continuum as is appropriate to the group we are working with.

The training sub-text

Every training event has its text and its sub-text. The text comprises the content of the training experience, and the strategies used to communicate that content to the learner. The sub-text involves a set of dynamics integral to the interaction of the trainer with the learners as individuals and as a group. Such dynamics exist in all forms of training and teaching, whatever their location on the developmental continuum. One of the ways that active learning moves along the continuum towards self-awareness is by challenging and exposing these dynamics: changing their status from sub-text to main text.

Active Learning: A Trainer's Guide deals primarily with the sub-text of the training scenario. We focus on the processes which underlie the strategies, activities and exercises that are the manifestation of the active learning philosophy and of the principles listed above. These processes concern the interface between trainer and learner, and their joint construction of an effective learning environment. We explore how these processes operate, the effects they are designed to have, and the responses that they can generate in the unsuspecting learner.

We also focus on the implications of these processes on the trainer. Most trainers have little experience of learning actively. Their early and formative experiences are likely to be ones in which they learned passively from a schoolteacher who was unwilling to share power or responsibility. The same is true for most adult learners. The transition away from this role-model towards an alternative relationship between teacher and learner takes place on many levels. The 'chalk and talk' trainers mentioned above, in the midst of their transition to a participative style, were coming to understand the different kinds of involvement and behaviour that were appropriate to the implementation of their facilitation method. They were coming to realise that it is not just a matter of using the right activities. The practical construction of an active learning scenario through activities and exercises needs to be underwritten by an understanding of the trainer's own needs for authority and power, and by an understanding of the intrinsic reluctance of the learner to enter into a new learning paradigm, where they are being asked to respond in unfamiliar ways.

How this book works

Having recognised what we wanted our writing to achieve, we also recognised that this would be difficult to realise in a book which consisted solely of straightforward prose. We felt this would lose some of the immediacy of our initial discussion, as well as assuming an authority that undermined our learning philosophy. Straight prose would create the relationship between us and you that we work to avoid in the training scenario. You would be passive, confronted by the unassailable authority of the authors. We didn't want this. If the book is to be a useful resource, it must engage you as actively as is possible in discussion and reflection on the issues involved.

In order to mitigate the innate authority of a book, we have chosen to use a variety of writing formats, partly because we thought the variety itself would be stimulating and challenging and partly because the different formats we chose could achieve different desired effects. This variety means that the book can be read in a number of ways. We will describe the various formats and intentions of each section now, to enable you to decide whether you want to start at the beginning and read through chronologically to the end, or work out a route which is more appropriate to your needs.

Dialogue

Section Two and Section Four are both in the form of an edited dialogue of a series of conversations that we had concerning specific issues. The dialogue format allows us to retain the dynamic of sharing and comparing which we found so useful. It also makes clear that we are talking about real experiences, and that the points we make are a result of those experiences. We are practitioners, not theorists. The dialogue demonstrates that our experience and our development are personal to us. We are not striving for objective truth. We are only striving to understand ourselves and the way we operate, in the hope that this will be relevant to you and your experience.

Section Two, *From the trainer's perspective*, concerns personal issues specific to the trainer:

- the development of power and authority;
- the importance of intuition;
- the boundaries of responsibility.

Section Four, *Learners are only human*, concerns personal issues specific to the learner but integral to the work of the trainer:

- needs and motivation;
- resistance;
- challenge.

Discussion of each issue leads to a set of activities which enable you to reflect on your response to our discussion and your relationship to the issue in question.

Prose

Section Three, *Training as a professional development*, is a 'straight prose' section which explores the relationship between professional and personal development, and the potential tension between the needs of the trainer and the needs of the learner. We spent much time debating the meanings of the words professional, personal and development, and the agendas and expectations that accompany these meanings. This section explores elements of the training experience which link professional and personal within a developmental continuum. We identify five key elements which cater for the immediate needs of professional development whilst at the same time laying the foundations from which development can continue beyond the confines of the training experience. This development, by its very continuance, incorporates the personal as well as the professional.

Activity

Section Five, *Managing your own development*, contains a series of activities built round the five elements detailed in Section 3. The activities provide you with a structured opportunity to reflect on and review your experience as a trainer, and to plan proactively for your future development.

Reportage

Section Six, *The elements in action*, is a journalistic account of a one-day course that Jill ran for a group of teachers and advisers with training responsibilities from one local education authority. The day took place after the main body of the book had been written, and Jill experimented with basing the structure for the course around the five elements. The section gives details of how the day went, and in particular details of the activities used to enable the group to experience the five elements at first-hand.

Narrative

Preceding all these sections is the first section of the book — a narrative account of what we think of as a typical training experience. It is a composite of experiences that we have both had, but we can only say with any certainty that it is typical to us. It may differ in several ways from *your* typical training experience.

We use the narrative opening because we feel that it effectively introduces several of the sub-text issues that we want to deal with. It does so in a way that locates these issues within a recognisable scenario that you can relate to your own experience. It will also give you, before you get too enmeshed in any false assumptions, a picture of the nature

of the training that we have both been involved in. The story is typical
of the life of an external trainer, working with a group who are
strangers, and who may never be seen again. If, for example, you work
on an on-going basis with the staff of a commercial organisation or a
local authority department, you may need to accommodate the differences in the nature of our work as preparation for your further reading
of the book.

Language

Some points about language and vocabulary:

1 To avoid problems with he/she pronouns, we have used they
   even when it refers back to a singular (eg even though the participant does . . . they may feel . . .).
2 To avoid being preclusive, we refer to 'the training event' and
   intend this to include all kinds of situation where learning is
   being facilitated by a trainer.
3 To avoid monotonous repetition, we sometimes refer to training
   events as courses, although we recognise that this may not be
   appropriate for some readers.
4 We have called people who attend training events variously
   learners and participants, although we recognise that readers
   may use other words.

In general, we found that existing vocabulary was not extensive
enough. We often found that words didn't exist to label what we were
trying to say. We spent a long time, for instance, trying to find a word
we both felt happy with to describe the fifth element in Section Three.
We finally settled reluctantly on *reflection*, only because it captured
our meaning slightly better than *evaluation*. So if there are times when
we appear to be using words repetitively, we apologise!

It seems that an adequate vocabulary does not yet exist for dealing
with the sphere of structured adult learning, and particularly learner-
centred learning. We went round asking people what words they use
to describe various things, only to be met with their pet problem! For
example, Hank was asked to find an alternative word for feedback, and
failed. We haven't tried to develop a language which adequately
describes the subtle actions and interactions which take place in the
training scenario (and we wish there was a viable alternative to training
scenario!), in case it turns out to be unintelligible jargon. But we hope
that a language is developed soon!

Section One: Par For The Course

She parked the car and sat quietly for a moment, trying to relax, to arrive. She was early, and it was barely daylight, a cold February morning. She dragged her briefcase over from the passenger seat, took a deep breath and opened the door. She walked slowly through the car park to the glass swing doors.

Inside, the manager of the training centre was waiting for her. He was relieved to see her, walked over to her, shook her hand, said hello. He was at her disposal. For a while. He couldn't come on the course, unfortunately, he would have liked to have. 'You know how it is — but if there's anything you need, please don't hesitate . . .' She smiled, asking to see the rooms that were available, knowing that movement would calm her down, that choices, decisions to be made, would energise her.

The man, also glad to be on the move, to be contributing, led her to the rooms that he had earmarked for the course. There were two. Neither of them was ideal. This was not unusual. There were only a few rooms in the building that provided the right kind of environment: the right size, light, atmosphere, furniture, quiet, and she didn't have priority. There were other courses. Today the choice was typical. One room far too big. The other just too small. One room too formal. The other too comfortable. As soon as she walked into the large room, a converted school hall, the parqué floor and stacked plastic chairs an uncomfortable reminder, she knew that she couldn't work here. Unless she had to. She asked to see the other room, politely, because she knew the man had assumed that the course would be run from his main hall. He had even asked the caretaker to put some flowers on one of the tables set out at one end of the room.

The other room was in another building within the centre, the same building as the dining area and bar. It was much smaller. It would be difficult to fit 40 people in here. It had a carpet. There were some cumbersome soft chairs grouped round low coffee tables. But there *were* wall display boards. And it had started to rain. She didn't want to get wet trooping outside at mealtimes, and neither would anybody else. Extra chairs would have to be found, but the atmosphere was relaxed, and the lack of space could be turned to advantage, pushing people closer together, encouraging them to co-operate, to feel part of a group.

She felt that she was being an inconvenience, but he agreed to the change with good grace, promising to find the extra chairs from somewhere. Before he went, she checked on the equipment she had asked for — the flip-charts and the audio-visual equipment that she wanted to be available all week. The manager looked at her blankly. She smiled at him with effort, explaining the need for access to the equipment at all times during the course, explaining that she had made this clear both over the phone and in writing prior to the course. He said that he would see what he could do. She was most grateful. He left her quickly to make the necessary arrangements.

Left alone in the room, she spent a few minutes getting used to it — the space, the atmosphere. She pulled a table away from the wall, and dragged it across the room. She put her briefcase on the table. She stood looking over the empty chairs. Just enough room. A bit tight. She looked at her watch. Soon she would be past the point of no return. Now she just wanted to sag, to sit down, to rest for a moment. To pretend that she had a choice. Right now, everything felt like an effort.

Leaving her case, she went in search of someone who would help her carry the boxes of material in from the boot of the car. She found the caretaker, and as they walked back through the car park, she explained to him that the furniture in the room would be moved around and reorganised in many different ways during the week and could it, please, be left as it was from day to day? She had run courses here before where the cleaners had come in and rearranged things each evening. The caretaker suggested that she negotiate with the cleaners as the week progressed. He seemed interested — 'Not the usual type of course, then?'. She made a mental note to invite the caretaker to join the course one evening. One of the principles of the course was about being considerate of other people's needs. The caretaker would be able to give the participants some feedback about how they behaved in relation to him and his staff. She felt pleased with herself. She was beginning to function.

She was laughing with the caretaker when her co-trainer arrived. She presented him with the decision about the room. There was not the time now for any discussion. She suggested that they rearrange the tables and chairs and make the room look as purposeful and welcoming as possible.

The chairs were arranged in rows in front of the table she had moved. She had thought about the arrangement carefully. The course was about dealing with change. Maybe the way the furniture was arranged at the beginning of the course should signify this by being set out in an unfamiliar way. Not in the standard rows that people expect at the beginning of courses, but in small groups randomly distributed throughout the room. This would also challenge any possible assumptions that the participants might have about the nature of their participation. They were not going to sit in rows, listening to her, passive recipients of knowledge.

But she had decided against this strategy. People might feel suspicious, threatened, even cynical, if they came in and saw the chairs arranged in groups. They would probably rearrange them into rows anyway, deliberately resisting any attempt at non-conformity, or maybe just assuming that the caretaker hadn't done his job. She felt it would be more effective to allow them the familiar as they walked in, and then ask them to rearrange the furniture themselves, as part of an activity. Less threatening, anyway.

When they had finished arranging the furniture, she went out into the foyer to see how many people had turned up. There were only ten minutes now until the course was due to start. When she had first arrived she had been aware of a few people hanging around the coffee machine in the foyer. She had deliberately not paid them too much attention, preferring to get the practical details sorted out before switching her focus on to people.

Now, surreptitiously, she had a look, just to get an idea of what they were like, not wanting to introduce herself yet. There were about fifteen people in the foyer, and she could see through the doors that a number of cars were pulling into the car park. She quickly scanned the fifteen. Most of them were men. Masculine-looking men, muscular, big. They all seemed to have beards! Her first instinct was to run away. She forced herself to take a second look, and this time she saw the few women present in the room, hidden amongst the dominating males. And the men didn't all have beards, even if they did seem to fill the available space. She felt less intimidated. A bit less intimidated.

She returned to the room to sit down, calm down, collect herself for a few minutes. She was supposed to have brought back some coffee for herself and her co-trainer, but she had forgotten. He went to get his own coffee. She was glad to be on her own for a few minutes, to run over how she was going to introduce the course, how she was going to get people going. Her co-trainer understood this need, and left her alone. There would be time later in the day to discuss the sessions he would be responsible for.

As she sat there, people started to drift in. The women came first, carefully choosing seats and preparing themselves, finding their notebooks and pens. Some men were coming in now. They didn't look quite as big as they had seemed to her when she saw them en masse in the foyer. That one had a nice face. He smiled at her, she was pleased to smile back. A large bearded man strode in, walking right across to the far side of the room, ostentatiously taking his jacket off before sitting down. She decided against making a point of saying hello to him, even though he had been the only one to avoid acknowledging her existence in any way. Now a clump of men came in, loudly joking and talking. Some of them broke away to go and sit with the man on the far side. The others dispersed around the room, seeking out colleagues or friends.

She looked at her watch. She was waiting for the arrival of the man who had organised the course: the director of the department that all the participants worked for. He was late, but then, in all of the numerous planning meetings they had had, he had always been late. He had always kept her waiting. She had never made an issue of it. Now she wished she had. He came into the room, smiling at her as he took up a position in front of her table. He wished her good morning before turning to face the group.

He had insisted on coming to make a formal introduction to the course. Generally she preferred to do without these 'ceremonies'. They were usually pointless, often counter-productive. She had got tired, over the years, of introductions which said things like 'We are pleased to have the experts here to tell us how we should be doing things!' or 'I have been on courses with these trainers before and I know you are going to enjoy the experience!'. They threw up barriers which could take most of the first session to break down. This time she had told the man how she wanted to be introduced. And to his credit, he did what she asked. Now it was her turn.

She had watched the group carefully while their boss had done his bit. Their mood had changed as soon as he walked in. They fell quiet. Not a respectful silence, but not a sullen one either. More passive and resigned than anything else. There didn't seem to be a great bond between the director and his staff. And, by the way he was making sure that they knew that it was only because of him that the course was happening at all, she could understand why. It was usually impossible to predict the relationship between course participants and course organiser — one of the reasons she preferred to do without the 'introductory remarks'. Here it was evident that the relationship was not that healthy, and now that she had been firmly associated with the director in the eyes of the participants she was going to have to make sure that she disassociated herself quickly. And do so without offering herself as a receptacle for their resentment. Not easy.

Having sensed that the energy level in the room had slumped during the formal introduction, she decided to get the course organiser out of the room as quickly as possible. She stood up and moved forward, so that she was closer to the group, and between them and their director. She thanked him for his introduction, explaining to the group that he would not be staying for the rest of the course. The man took the hint. He stood up, made a half-hearted joke that didn't work, and left, saying goodbye to her as he backed towards the door.

As soon as the door was closed behind him, she raised the tempo. She moved across to where her colleague was sitting, saying, 'Right then!' loudly and cheerfully. She put her hand on her colleague's shoulder in order to introduce him, but also to introduce a sense of contact and intimacy into the room. Then she talked for about five minutes so that people could relax and acclimatise to her manner, her voice, her way of speaking. She wanted them to tune into the energy level she was giving out, because that was the energy level she was going to be demanding of them. She went through the objectives and principles of the course, emphasising that everyone would need to become actively involved, that they would be learning from each other as much as from her, and that 'taking responsibility for your own learning' was one of the central themes of the course. As she was talking, she smiled at them a lot, giving reassurance.

When she had said all that she needed to say, she shifted gear again turning down the volume, and speaking more slowly. She asked the group to get up off their chairs, and move around the room. She told them to spend a few minutes finding out about the other people on the course, who they were, what section of the department they were from, and why they had chosen, or had been chosen, to come on the course. She asked them to remember the names of six people that they hadn't met before. This was the crunch time: anything could happen;

people could quite simply turn round and say no. After years of being a trainer, she was never going to find this an easy moment.

There was an embarrassed silence. She could feel the group, who had gradually warmed to her through her introduction, go cold again. They didn't move. Her co-trainer, who had stood up, on cue, when she had given the instruction, moved towards someone on the first row. There was a reluctant shuffling of feet and chairs. She thought, 'Come on. Please get up!' A man at the back stood up. It was the big bearded man she had picked out earlier. In his deep, resonant voice, he boomed out:

'I was asked to do this at a church meeting last week. I didn't like it then. And I won't do it now!'

The room went quiet. People stopped their tentative movement, or sat still on their seats. They all turned to look at her. She too froze, for a second, staring at the man. Then she looked around the rest of the group, waiting to see if anybody else was going to speak. They all looked back at her, waiting to see what she was going to do, how she was going to respond to this outright challenge. She turned back towards the man, meeting his eye. 'Ok,' she said. 'Do other people feel the same way?' Several voices said 'yes' strongly. Other people didn't say anything, not prepared to commit themselves either way. She felt as if the group were testing her out. They wouldn't back down. But she had to find a way of asserting her authority.

She explained, again, why she had asked them to do that activity. She told them that the way she worked as a trainer was to involve people in the process, and that meant that they were active, literally moving around the room, meeting people, talking to them, working together. She asked for suggestions about how that could be done in a way that they found acceptable. Having challenged her, and having their challenge accepted, the group responded to this request. They might not have. They might have seen it as weakness. But they didn't. They said that they were willing to work with other people, but they were not prepared to play games. They felt that having to remember six new names was childish, that she was treating them like children. They suggested that she should have asked them to turn to the people they were sitting next to and talk to them.

'Thank you,' she said. 'Perhaps we could all do that now then, please.' But she knew that they would just turn into their cliques and make no effort to get to know people that they hadn't met before. Which was why . . . She let it go. It had been her mistake. She had read the climate, she had known what was going on, she had seen the cliques forming, she had felt the response to the director, the sullen resistance. She had pushed too hard, too early, and they had dug their heels in. To have fought them would have made things worse. Better to let them feel that they had some power in the situation, to see that she was flexible but that she wasn't weak. And try and break through their defences later, more gradually, try and get them to open up.

★   ★   ★   ★   ★

By the afternoon, there had been some significant movement. Her calm self-assertion that morning had earned her the respect of the group, even though she had appeared to let them have their way. They were now working in new groupings, with three or four people that they didn't know beforehand and the existing cliques and power bases were breaking down. On the morning of the next day, the small groups would be presented with their main task for the course: to visit the different offices within their department and carry out some research into their staff development needs. Each office had representatives on the course, and it was important for future relationships to have mixed groups working on the task. But nobody was going to research their own office. The practical arrangements had been made before the course. The groups had to plan how they were going to work together and carry out a task which, given the political climate within the organisation, was extremely sensitive.

The most challenging aspect of the task for the participants was forming a working relationship with people that they had only just met. Some of the teams got on very well, quickly establishing a supportive climate. Others struggled. One group in particular got stuck in planning how they were going to tackle the task. In the end she had to intervene, working with them to identify what was going wrong. It transpired that they had spoken to one of the representatives from the office they were working on, and had gained the impression that they would have a hostile reception when they went in to interview staff. They didn't want to do it.

She called all the teams together so that they could compare notes on their planning, and take stock of how far they had got. As part of the stock-take, she asked them all to recall the information they had given one another about their own office, and to consider how helpful it was, given what they had discovered about the nature of the task whilst they had been planning. Out of this came a re-evaluation of the purpose of the exercise, and what was achievable in the time they had available. Most of the teams readjusted their targets as a result. This sharing of information also showed that everyone was feeling anxious about doing the task. People became more supportive of each other, giving more useful information about their offices, being reassuring, offering encouragement. The whole group came together for the first time on the course.

When the exercise was completed, the teams had to make some form of presentation to the rest of the group, based on things that they had learnt as a result of their research. The presentation had to be given in an active way, involving the group as much as possible in learning from each team's experience, and also involving them in reflecting on what they had learnt from each presentation. It was a complicated task, and a challenging one in a number of ways, not least because of the exposure of standing up in front of your colleagues.

Most of the groups responded well. One group didn't. Or rather one man didn't. He didn't stick to plan. When it was his turn to speak, he improvised. He missed out some stages in the presentation, and introduced some unplanned and more complicated concepts. What he did was interesting, but it completely threw the woman coming next. When she presented a set of questions to help the group reflect on the presentation, the questions no longer fitted what had gone before. She stuck to the plan, but it didn't work any more. And she was furious. The man couldn't see the problem. The group became confused and irritated. Tempers were getting frayed.

She waited for a while to see how the group would handle the conflict, how they would help the man and woman resolve things. But they were tired. Some of them had done their presentations, others were waiting to do theirs. So in the end she intervened, asking the team to focus on what they could learn from the experience, rather than on apportioning blame for why things had gone wrong. People stopped in their tracks, surprised, embarrassed. And then the learning points came out: changing things on the spur of the moment affects the people you are working with; too much too quick makes it more difficult for the learner; in the woman's words: 'If the first fence is too high, people won't get over it!'. And that you can cut through conflict by asking people to focus on the positive, rather than getting stuck on interpreting the negative.

*   *   *   *   *

On the fourth day of the course the group was going to be visited by their director, so that they could relay to him the findings of their research into the staff development needs of the department. At first they thought she was joking, and laughed when she told them. Then they realised that she wasn't, and became angry. They didn't trust their director. He wouldn't take any notice, it was a waste of time. Or he would use what they said against them after the course. It was too great a risk. They wouldn't do it.

She was surprised. She hadn't realised the relationship with the director was so bad. And she was disappointed. She had thought that they would trust her enough by now to know that she wasn't going to set them up in any way. She told them bluntly that the director was coming after lunch, which gave them two hours to plan what they were going to do. She suggested that they spend part of their time planning what they felt safe in saying, and what they felt was too risky. Alternatively, they could use the opportunity to try and establish a more trusting relationship with their director. Above all, it was an experience from which both they and their director could learn.

They spent the two hours arguing amongst themselves about what was best. Different views of the director came out. He wasn't that bad. He was. Different views of what to do were expressed. Some people wanted to elect a spokesperson. Others wanted to write a statement and present it to him when he came in. Some wanted to be aggressive and ask direct and awkward questions. One or two wanted to ignore him, others wanted to make the most of the opportunity to get to know him better. She listened and said little, simply reminding them of how much time they had left, and when asked, saying that she wasn't joking and that he really was coming. She asked them whether somebody was going to go and meet him, and how they were going to make him feel welcome. And they went on arguing and missed lunch while they debated what to do.

He arrived on time. Somebody went to meet him in the foyer and brought him to the room, maintaining superficial conversation about the weather. A chair had been placed for him within the circle that they had formed. A slight space had been left either side of him. She had explained to him beforehand that it was important to let the group take responsibility for initiating the discussion, and that the atmosphere would probably be tense to begin with. He had said that he was willing to take the risk, but she could see now that he was feeling very nervous. There was a hiatus and no-one spoke. One woman sat there with her eyes shut for the entire time that he was there! Then people began to ask him the questions that they had prepared and agonised over. He replied carefully and at length, taking control of the exchanges, asking questions of the group, some of which no-one could answer. It was a nerve-racking experience for everybody.

After the director had gone, she held a post-mortem. How did they feel about it? People were confused, some a bit shame-faced, others angry. She asked them a series of questions, debriefing them as if they had just been on a flying mission. They discussed the questions in their small groups. They knew that they had shifted responsibility, had given over control, had given him most of the power in the situation. They saw that they had done that. They recognised that he had been nervous, unsure, unconfident of his reception. And they hadn't helped him. They realised that they had come to see him in a particular way, and that they had refused to adjust this perspective when they were confronted with him on a personal level. They acknowledged that if you don't take risks, things stay the same. And they accepted that they had failed to support each other, to use each other and draw strength from each other. They were surprised when the woman who had kept her eyes closed said that it had been the only way she could cope with the situation. Nobody had even noticed. And they certainly hadn't given her an opportunity beforehand to share her feelings and find a way of being more comfortable. They realised that they had operated independently, as a group of individuals, in a situation which required co-operation, support and encouragement.

The course was nearly over. She suggested that they spend the rest of the time available in looking at what they had learnt, and how it could be used in the future. She told them to go back to the beginning of the course. Forget about the visit they had just received. Remember what happened first, and what happened after that and so on. She got them, in their groups, to draw up a timetable of what had happened on the course, and against each event to write down how they had felt at the time. Gradually the group cheered up, remembering what they had been through, laughing, feeling good about themselves. She asked people to make notes about things they had learnt from the different tasks and activities, and to compare notes in their groups. She asked people to identify some key learning points that they would try and use when they went back to work. She asked them to plan how they were going to apply these learning points, to plan specific actions that they could take to reinforce or further develop their learning.

People worked hard, pushed each other, giving each other feedback, promising support. She went round each of the groups to see how open people were being, both with themselves, and with each other. She was pleased. They were setting themselves challenging tasks. One group planned to arrange a meeting with the director to discuss staff development issues. They had been disturbed by the degree of their own prejudice, in their investment in seeing him as a 'baddy'. They wanted to do something about it. They thought that the results of their research had been valuable, and it was ridiculous not to communicate them properly.

The man with the beard who had challenged her at the beginning was less committed. He had struggled during the course, maintaining his mood of resistance. He had never fully engaged in the activities, and during mealtimes she had overheard him complaining about the course, about how he couldn't see the point. As everybody else had become more involved and relaxed, he had become increasingly isolated. He had made efforts to contribute, and hadn't caused any more difficulty. But now, as he reflected on the course, he was struggling to find any value in the experience. His group were pushing him to be more positive, to identify one thing that he had learnt from the course, but it was having the opposite effect. She suggested that they leave him alone for a while. She asked him whether he felt uncomfortable at the moment. He said that he did, he didn't want to feel so negative, but he couldn't see the point of it all. She suggested that he stay with the discomfort, and try to keep an open mind. She told him to listen to what other people were saying, and to see if that helped him to understand things better. And then she moved on to another group.

★   ★   ★   ★   ★

The course was over, and people were getting ready to go. She sat at the table, putting things into her briefcase. People came up to say goodbye and to thank her. Not all of them. Some just left, anxious to avoid the traffic, or already preoccupied with going back into the world. The man with the beard came and thanked her for being so patient with him. He said he was sorry if he had been difficult. She smiled and said that it was OK. He was the last to leave. She sat there for a few minutes looking at the room, feeling tired and sad, deciding whether to put the chairs back in rows, or leave them as they were. She left them, and went out to find the centre director to thank him for his help during the week.

It was only when she had driven out of the car park that she realised that she had forgotten to ask the caretaker to join the course on the Wednesday evening. What a shame! Waste of a good idea.

Section Two: From The Trainer's Perspective

Introduction

The story in Section One is typical, in most respects, of experiences we have both had as trainers. It doesn't always happen like that! We don't always get such a direct challenge at the beginning of every course, thankfully! But the story graphically illustrates several of the issues that we will be exploring in this book.

We started with the story because it introduces these issues from the perspective of the trainer. It introduces the emotional sub-text of the trainer's job. In other sections we will be exploring some of the key elements in the training process. In this section, we are focusing on the *implications* of being a trainer. In other words, we are focusing on the demands that being a trainer makes on us as people.

In our experience, being a trainer has frequently involved travelling a long way to work in unfamiliar surroundings with a group of people whom we don't know and in some cases will probably never see again. It is a lonely, insecure, often thankless job. It continually involves overcoming feelings of isolation and anxiety, drawing on reserves of energy, holding on to a belief in our personal competence, finding once again a sense of our power, both personal and professional. It involves walking out in front of a sea of strange faces, and rapidly coming to understand why those faces are there, what they want, and how we need to be to ensure that they get it.

We may be assured of our technical ability to create a climate that is conducive to learning. We may be confident in the material and the processes that we are working with. But at a base level, we are just one person confronted by a group of other people who have an expectation that we are going to 'do' something to them! Technique alone is no guarantee that we are going to be able to respond to these people effectively. The content of a course will not necessarily motivate them, nor ensure that they will respect our authority, or have confidence in our ability.

Section Two explores some of the issues that lie behind the technical business of being a trainer. It focuses on three areas:

1 The development of power and authority
2 The importance of intuition
3 The boundaries of responsibility

It is a response to some of the questions we asked ourselves when we first planned the book: where does a trainer's power come from? Why are they granted authority? How important is intuition in the training context? To what extent are they responsible for the welfare and development of the people who attend their courses?

We are exploring these questions now in order to establish a principle which underlies all other sections of the book: the need for the trainer to regard themselves as a developing individual, and to regard the business of being a trainer as a process of personal development. This is based on the belief that only if a trainer is actively engaged in their own development can they effectively contribute to the development of others.

We have used the questions that we identified above as a structure for reflecting on and interpreting our own experience as trainers. We are responding to the issues personally because they are personal issues. We are resisting the illusion of right answers.

Section Two is an edited transcript of a conversation between the two of us. It is divided into three chapters, each dealing with one of the issues listed above. At the end of each chapter there is a summary which leads into a set of activities which you can use to reflect on the chapter, and to relate its content to your own situation and experience.

1 Power and authority

The discussion starts with the issue of power and authority. What kind of power does a trainer exercise in the training situation, and how is that power perceived? Is there a power that stems from the position of being a trainer? Or from the knowledge or experience that the trainer possesses? Or does it come more from the power of the trainer's personality? And what is the difference between power and authority?

H: You were a teacher for twelve years, before you started training teachers in active tutorial work. Did you use that experience to establish your authority as a trainer?

J: I wanted to show people that I was just the same as them. I had done what they were doing now. I knew about it. I knew what it was like. I didn't want people to use my position as the director of a national training organisation as the basis for me working with them. So I wanted to say, 'I'm just like you really,' and try to establish more of an equal relationship from the start. I was more concerned with my credibility than my authority. But I also wanted to make clear that I wasn't there now. I wanted to show that I had first-hand experience, but also that I had stood back, taken a more objective look, thought about it, developed my ideas. I don't feel the need to do all that any more, though.

H: Is that because you feel more confident, more secure in your own abilities as a trainer?

J: I came to realise that people do acknowledge my expertise. I don't feel I have to justify it now, or apologise for it. I might as well use it. I don't want to pretend that I don't have it. That wouldn't be honest. It would be a con. It could just end up confusing people, or being counter-productive. I came to realise that you can't deny your power if it's there. Whatever kind of power it is, you can't hide it, or pretend it doesn't exist. Even power of position. What people saw me doing was rejecting their attempts to give me recognition for that power. They didn't thank me for rejecting them.

H: I wonder what people are doing when they want to give you recognition for your power of position, and are disappointed if you don't accept it. I'm thinking of a situation that arises on a three-day course that I'm involved in running at the moment. There are three of us involved as trainers, but one of us is there not because of her training skills, but because she is an acknowledged expert in the particular field that the course deals with. And people were foisting power of position onto her, as if her presence was some kind of endorsement for them: 'If she's here, I must be learning something!' I wonder how important that kind of endorsement is in the end. I think that power of position can obstruct real learning, because it impedes the independence of the learner. It can serve as a screen, and then people have the option to hide behind it, rather than to find things out for themselves.

J: I think a trainer operates more effectively from the power of their personality. Then people have to deal with them on face value, and are not preconditioned to accept everything as gospel. And in the end you have to earn their respect anyway, whatever your position might lead you to expect. You have to actually go out and earn the respect of the group.

H: The difference between authority and power, to me, is that power is inherent in the person, or in their situation, whereas authority is afforded to you by other people. It is a decision that they make for themselves: whether to grant you authority or not. And whatever power you have, whether it is power of position, or knowledge, or personality, there's no guarantee that you'll be granted authority by a group. If you've been put in a position of power by being the leader of a course, you could continue to exercise power by being prescriptive, couldn't you? By telling them what to do and what to learn. But you wouldn't necessarily be granted any authority by the group. People might kowtow to your power. But they would find your use of power oppressive, and so they would resist it. Even if the only form of resistance available to them was not to learn. To make sure you failed.

J: A teacher that I trained came up to me at the end of a course once and said: 'What you're about is shifting the locus of power in the classroom, aren't you?'. And that seemed such a succint way of putting it. Traditionally, learners (children *and* adults) have so little power in the learning situation. They are told what they are going to learn and how they are going to learn it. There is no consideration about whether it's of any use to them, or how best it could be presented to them to enable them to learn. And, as a trainer, once you stop drawing on the power that comes from simply being the trainer, the holder of knowledge, you are thrown back onto yourself as an individual. You need to be powerful to share power in a learning situation, to say: 'I don't know it all, your experience is as important as mine, you have a say in what happens next'.

H: Are you saying, then, that you have to develop a new kind of authority with a group, one that isn't based on you being the all-powerful one?

J: I think that I actually strive, from the moment I stand up at the beginning of a course, to earn authority. And that is such hard work, isn't it? Because, whatever your power base is, you have to do more. You have to contribute effectively from your power. Power is what you start with. It's how you use it that will give you authority, or not. And I think people need to see very quickly how you intend to use your power.

H: I think people look for two things. From me, anyway. The first is energy. I think people want to know that I have energy and can provide energy. And, secondly, I think they want evidence that I have an intuitive empathy with the group which will provide them with the motivation, or the incentive, to give me authority. Because in some way they feel that I have the intuitive ability to care for them in some way.

J: But you have to work at that. I know when I stand up after I've been introduced, there is just literally a sea of faces. I don't know anything about them. They are anonymous. Intuition and empathy with them doesn't come about automatically, does it?

H: What I try and do, and I've only recently become aware that it's what I do, is to receive the messages they are sending. I try to be alive to the atmosphere in the room. To open my intuitive chan-nels, if you like, so that I am receiving information. And then what I do depends on that information. I know that sounds vague, but what I used to do was worry about *me*. I used to spend that time at the beginning working out what I was going to do, how I was going to be, how I wanted to come across. It would make me tight and anxious. And I wouldn't be aware of what was going on around me. I would stand up to speak, and my eyes wouldn't be making contact, they would be sliding over the faces in front of me as if we were separated by a glass panel. And the effect was that I wouldn't be there for them, in the present. I would be there for me. And what they would pick up on was that I was concerned about me, and my energy wasn't available. So now I try consciously to stay open to them, and in some way to signal that openness.

J: Can you think of a specific instance which illustrates some of this?

H: I'm thinking of a course I helped run for a group of trainers from a police force. I was quite anxious about doing it, worried about what they would be like, and whether they would reject me, or whether my prejudices would get in the way, you know. I went to the venue early so that I could have time to be around the group as they waited for the course to start. I forced myself to become aware of them as individuals, to focus on the differences within the group, the different faces, the different clothes, the different accents, to stop me from lumping them all together in one big stereotype. I remember there was one guy there who was wearing white sneakers. And I felt much more relaxed, much more available because of that time. I needed to, in order to get a sense of my own authority in relation to the group.

J: Do you find, once you've established your authority with a group, that that's it, you've got it for good?

H: Generally, yes. I think those first few minutes are crucial. But it depends on the strength of the group, the strength of their culture. And that depends on how well they know each other beforehand. This group all knew each other. Their culture was very male, very jokey. I spent a lot of time in the beginning trying to interrupt that culture, to find a way in that wouldn't compromise me. It was like working out a balance of giving them just enough of it without letting it get out of hand. If I hadn't accepted it at all, they would not have allowed me in, they wouldn't have given me any authority. I felt that I had to demonstrate my ability to empathise with their culture. Only then would they allow me to take them outside of it. At the end of the course, I was wrapping things up, standing in the middle of a group of maybe forty people summarising where they'd got to, and somebody cracked a joke, and I automatically retorted with a joke. They just fell about laughing and somebody said, 'That's better Hank. That's more like it'. And then they all really fell about laughing — to a quite extraordinary degree. I've never known anything like it. It was as if all along, they wanted that final acceptance of their culture, they wanted me finally to show that I thought it was all right. I think their need of my acceptance was an indication of the authority I had built up through the course.

J: It puts me in mind of a number of occasions when the culture of a group has threatened my authority, even when it is quite a positive, happy culture. I came up with a formula for the times when I felt 'enough's enough,' or 'I've got to get a grip'. I used to say at an appropriate point: 'Look, there are thirty of you, and only one of me and you're making it very difficult for me,' and there have been times when the atmosphere's changed, just like that. The difficulty is knowing when is the appropriate time to say it, to say: 'Look, I've gone along with you to this point but if I am to continue to help the course to proceed, you've got to change things slightly'. There is a risk there that they will just reject you, and so the timing is crucial.

H: Do you think it is harder for you because you are a woman? Are men more reluctant to let you in, to give you authority?

J: It certainly adds another dimension. Most of the time I have co-trained with men, so I'm not a woman on my own. But there have been occasions where there is an automatic assumption by the person who is formally introducing the course at the beginning that the man will start things off. And then when I stand up, there is a slight resistance to the fact that it's a woman who is standing there and saying what the objectives and philosophy are and why they're there. I have to work quite hard at breaking down that resistance.

H: I find it hard to believe that they don't give you authority just through your power of personality. I would say you have a natural authority.

J: Well, this is where the intuitive relationship with the group starts. I can tell whether they see me as authoritative before I even open my mouth. I can sense resistance when I stand up to start, resistance to my being a woman or whatever. And there's a correlation between the degree of resistance that I am aware of and the amount of energy I put into it. I call it, 'going up a gear'. It's almost a conscious thing like taking in oxygen through three deep breaths. I read the faces when introductions are being made and I know at that point whether I need to go up a gear and put a terrific amount of energy into 'blazing'. There've been times when I've blazed at the audience to force my power of personality on them in order to be granted authority.

H: I sometimes have the opposite problem with the power of person-ality. Sometimes I'm aware that I'm blasting people, and I have to play it down. I know that my power of personality can be threaten-ing, can be counter-productive through intimidating or inhibiting people. It's taken quite a lot of feedback from people for me to really accept that that's true. I don't always believe that I am a powerful personality. I certainly don't always feel like one! And so I don't anticipate the effect. Also I think there are times when I'm insensitive to the effect that I'm having, usually when I'm nervous, and I overcome my nerves by performing and then realise that I'm overdoing it, to the detriment of other people.

J: I get nervous like that, but the effect it has on me is to be more reserved and gentle and to try and get people to recognise that I'm not going to threaten them or challenge them. But I have to over-lay that in the beginning with some kind of energy to get them going. My strategy is to smile a lot, almost make up to them as an audience. It is acting. It's not natural. I'm trying to be friends with them.

H: It sounds like you want to earn their acceptance, to be accepted by them. Whereas I think I'm motivated more by a need for applause. I'm not so concerned about being rejected by them. I'm more concerned about being ignored! And I mistrust that sometimes — I'm not sure that's what I should be after. But then if I didn't have that motivation, I guess I wouldn't get up there in the first place.

J: I'm not sure that it matters as long as you don't misuse it. As long as that's not all you want. As long as you don't exploit the situ-ation for your own ends. I wonder sometimes whether it is appro-priate to look for acceptance, whether that doesn't blur the edges of why I'm there. It doesn't do to be too nice, too cosy.

H: I'm getting better at being aware of my own needs and taking them into account. I used to try too hard at the beginning some-times, and people would find me overbearing or threatening. Mind you, there seem to be so many ways in which you can threaten people. By who you are, or what you ask of them. In the end any position of power, even the trainer's position, is a threat to the person who isn't in it.

J: Yes. There are times, when I split the group into pairs and there's been an odd one out, and I'll fill in as someone's partner. They suddenly realise that they're with the boss, and I'm amazed at how frightening they find that. You know, 'Oh, my goodness! You! But you're the teacher'. It's amazing how people insist on seeing you as powerful, however much you try and share the power in the situation with them. People don't always want to feel powerful. It brings too much responsibility. They may have an investment in the trainer holding on to the power. And that can clash with the trainer's investment in them being powerful, or at least, in them becoming powerful!

H: One of the things I'm aware of, in working out how powerful I need to be, is the need to understand how much power exists within the group. It's the balance of power that's important. I think one of the first things I do with a group is to try and reach some understanding of how powerful they are, so that I can work out the appropriate power-base for me. I'm thinking of a course I ran recently for a group of recreation managers. As they came in, I was aware of feeling that they were likely to want to appear powerful. They were all men and they were very physically imposing because they were all sportsmen of some kind. They didn't know each other, so there was no existing culture, but I found them quite intimidating, and there was a danger that I would over-compensate, over-exert my power as the trainer. But I had this strong feeling that I had to be careful not to be too powerful in relation to them, but just powerful enough to take them with me. It was a difficult balance. And when I did a contract of ground-rules with them at the beginning of the day, one of the ground-rules they wanted was to be able to criticise the course as it went along.

J: Was that one of the clues to their need for power?

H: Absolutely. It was very clear. And quite threatening, the way it was said. They had obviously had bad training experiences in the past! But I accepted it as a ground-rule. I made a point of welcoming it actually, but I also owned my nervousness about it. And it was as if that was all that needed to happen for them to feel powerful in the situation. They asked for, and were given, the licence to criticise the course. It would have been wrong of me to try to challenge that.

J: Did they ever criticise the course?

H: No. But I don't think that was totally to do with whether the course was any good or not. It was more about them exerting their power in relation to mine. By agreeing to their ground-rule, I met their needs around power. If I hadn't, they would have found ways to challenge me throughout the day, whether it was any good or not. Funnily, there was another kind of power issue going on that day. The person responsible for setting this course up was there as a participant. And he wanted *everybody* to know that he had been responsible for setting up the course! All day he was very noticeably doing things, like making sure that the tea came on time, and that the heating was right. I knew it wouldn't be worth me challenging the power he was claiming. It wasn't undermining my authority. And I felt that if I tried to shut him up, or if I ignored him, he would have found more and more disruptive ways of trying to get the recognition he wanted. So I gave him appreciation for what he did, in front of the group. And it was enough. I always try to accept that people have power, and need to feel powerful, however uncomfortable I find it at the time. I try not to compete with them, but that's hard, because my instinctive response is to compete, to perceive it as a threat. But I know that it's better to find ways in which they can get the recognition they need, preferably from the rest of the group.

J: There is a balance of power to try for, isn't there, whereby you can give people the power they need but retain enough within the room to carry on. And then there are times when the group lend you their power. There are times when the course has caused some turbulence and I am being challenged by one or two, or perhaps a small group of people. And because people are feeling disturbed, the challenge is unpleasant, aggressive. This happened last week actually. Somebody stood up, and very forcibly questioned the validity of what we were doing. I didn't see it coming, but as soon as it happened, I knew that it had been inevitable. It often happens to me like that. It's uncomfortable, because I'm being challenged and I'm losing power, and I can see that everyone else is sitting back to see what the outcome is going to be. And there's a moment at which I show that I'm helpless, to a degree. Then the balance of power in the room shifts and people give me power in order to deal with the challenge. It's usually a turning point for the whole course.

H: Do you do something to make that happen? To shift the power?

J: It's to do with showing that, at that moment, I feel helpless. And I do. I'm not pretending. It's got to be real. Sometimes I'm getting angry and having to really grit my teeth and hold the anger back. Or I'm feeling that I don't know what to do. And that feeling is communicated, somehow, to the majority of people out there. I look for signs amongst the group. I'm intuitively looking for help, really. If I sense at all that somebody wants to speak, I let them.

And almost 100% of the time they have been supportive.

H: Is it allowing yourself not to win?

J: Yes, but it's not conscious. By the time I realise what is happening, it's usually too late for me to do anything consciously about it. A lot of my power in the situation has already gone. I think it's just allowing my feelings to show, and not pretending that I'm in control of everything, because I'm not! I stand there waiting for the challenge to finish, and I show that I'm helpless. Or when it's finished, I might do something like letting a long pause go while I think, showing that I'm not sure how to answer this.

H: I'm aware when I'm in those situations that there's a bit of me that wants to resist the challenge, fight back, win. And I know that if I do, it will rebound on me later on in the course — they'll get their own back, or they'll find another way, or they won't be satisfied. But I don't want to lose the conflict because that will probably have as damaging a consequence. So it's allowing myself not to win it and to show that I don't need to win it. Not in a dismissive or belittling way. I do it by showing that I'm vulnerable in the situation, that I'm finding it difficult, that I'm not sure what to do. But there's a difference between being vulnerable and being weak, I think. And it's about getting to the point where you can allow yourself to be vulnerable without feeling weak. Then people see the strength of being vulnerable, in you being vulnerable.

J: That's it!

Summary

In this chapter, we have focused on the nature of power in the training situation. We have suggested that a move away from traditional teaching, where power is retained almost entirely by the teacher, means that trainers have to draw on their personality more than their position in order to have power in the learning situation.

Trainers who actively set out to 'shift the locus of power' may find that the learning group are initially resistant to that process. They may prefer the conventional teacher-pupil relationship to a more challenging relationship which demands the engagement of responsibility for self and others.

Being granted authority by a group is an essential stage in developing a power-sharing relationship. We became aware, as we talked, that from the beginning of a course, we take steps to 'earn' authority from the group. But we do it in different ways, and differently according to circumstances. We may need to go up a gear or down a gear, in terms of energy and input. We may need to sit still and show calm stability, or move around to show dynamic energy. But we know that we must earn authority before we can usefully proceed any further.

The process of sharing power involves continual adjustment. The locus of power is not static. It is fluid, moving between trainer and group depending on the nature of the learning and the personalities within the group. People unaccustomed to being given power in the learning situation may react by resisting or challenging. These reactions can put pressure on the trainer to reassert a power of position. We believe that the trainer can resist this pressure by revealing their vulnerability, and that this, in fact, is a key strategy in shifting the locus of power.

Activity

Below is a series of questions which you may wish to use as a structure for reflecting on your responses to the issues we have discussed in this chapter, and the ways in which they relate to your experience as a trainer.

- *What kind of power do you bring into your work as a trainer?*
  Do you have power of position — as an expert, or as a manager, or as part of an appraisal system, for example?
  Do you perceive your personality as a source of power for you as a trainer — if so how?
- *Does your power work for you or against you in training situations?*
  For example, does your power of position encourage or inhibit openness?
  For example, does your power of personality generate resistance or co-operation?
- *What steps do you take to develop authority at the beginning of a course?*
  It may help you to think back over how you behave at the beginning of a course in order to recognise which behaviours contribute to you being granted authority by the group.
- *Does the nature of your authority change as the course progresses?*
  If so, how does it change?
- *Do people resist or challenge your authority as a trainer?*

If so, how do you react to such behaviour? Do you, for example, tend to assert your power of position, or do you engage in debate with the individual or group, in order to persuade by power of knowledge or experience?

Comment

You may feel that these questions do not apply to your situation. Or you may feel that establishing authority is your greatest problem as a trainer. It is likely that most trainers will be somewhere between these two extremes. They will be aware of the need to earn authority. They will recognise where their power comes from, whether position or personality or a combination of the two. And they may find that their power makes it easy or difficult for them to gain authority from a group of learners.

Possibly you have to work against your position, or your reputation, or your personality, if you are to be effective with a particular group of learners. We have both been in situations when we have had to establish ourselves in spite of these things, which have been viewed with suspicion or resentment, or which have been experienced as intimidating or oppressive. We found, in talking, that we took quite deliberate steps to develop our authority with a group, but that those steps varied according to the demands of the particular situation. In the next chapter, we explore how we know what steps to take. But we found, in talking about power and authority, that we had one strategy in common, that of showing our vulnerability as a way of circumventing pressure to reassume power of position.

2 Intuition and instinct

In the previous chapter, we made frequent reference to our use of intuition and instinct in the training situation. So much so that we felt we should discuss why it was that we valued them so highly, and give over a chapter of the book to that discussion. First we defined what we each meant when we used those words.

J: When I talk about working from instinct, I mean a kind of 'feeling awareness' — an awareness that comes through the feelings that I am having. I talk about it in terms of reading the situation, understanding what's going on out there. And also in terms of timing responses or interventions.

H: I use intuition more in the sense of formulating responses. There are times when I'm not sure where my responses to certain situations have come from. I don't feel that I always consciously think things through. I get a flash of intuition which tells me what to do.

J: I was thinking more of times when I know what I am going to do next, but I have to feel out when people are ready to receive it. For example: the point at the end of my introduction when I ask people to get up off their chairs and rearrange themselves in the room. I use my instinct in knowing when is the right moment to bring the introduction to an end and in feeling when they're relaxed enough to go along with my demand that they move. It's about reading the faces and recognising that they know what's coming and not keeping them in suspense too long. So there's a precision about thinking, 'Now's the time. I'm going to stop talking and get them to move'. Sometimes it's sooner than I anticipated and most often it's later. But if I leave it too long it's really hard to get them out of their chairs.

H: I find it hard to assess when to stop whenever I talk for any length of time. It's not just that point at the beginning of the day. I often become aware that I've gone on for too long, and I've allowed them to settle into passivity. I can feel the atmosphere change, go heavy. And I know that I'll have to work harder to shift them out of it, and back into active engagement. What I find difficult is that I tend to get carried away when I talk in those situations. If people look as if they are interested in what I am saying, I get duped by that, and go on longer than I should.

J: I try always to keep that in the back of my mind. I find that I'll sometimes get drawn in by a question, and end up saying more than I'd intended. But I can now usually sense when people feel overloaded, and I'll stop automatically, without thinking. That's what I mean by instinctively reading the situation.

H: I ran a one-day workshop on communication skills for a team from a local authority. I ran it with another trainer. It became apparent, right at the beginning of the day, that what they needed was to resolve communication problems within the team. They were giving us all these signs. They kept getting up and going to the toilet, all the time through the morning. At one point, somebody got up to make coffee in the middle of an activity. So a lot of their energy was being refracted out of the room. And snide comments were being made, quite audibly. There was a lot of small-group conversation going on, so that people weren't listening to my colleague, who was leading the morning session. I felt that they were acting out their communication problems for me, as a way of directly involving me in them. So as the morning went on I became more and more aware that the team had serious problems. I could feel the tension in the room and the antipathy between people. If I was reading the situation, they were spelling it out for me, in big letters! But part of the situation was their attempt to embroil me in it. And that made it quite difficult to read things objectively. They were very frustrating, and I had to try hard to stay separate from them, to see it as their situation, and not join in. If I'd got angry with them, for example, that would have been joining in in a way that wouldn't have been useful to them.

J: So what did you do? How were you with them?

H: Well this is what I mean by an intuitive response. While they were doing activities, I found that I was walking round the outside of the group. Talking about it afterwards I said, without even think-ing about it, that I was 'corralling' the group. I was giving them a circumference within which they worked and I was trying, by that, to bind them together. I don't know where it came from. I certainly wasn't thinking that when I was doing it. But that's what I was doing, and it worked. It had an effect. There was a clear need to mark out the territory of their learning environment. And that had been purely an intuitive response based on my reading of a difficult situation.

J: I suppose that now you've described it, the point at which I ask people to get up and move about and find out who everyone is, is always one of the most difficult moments for them, and for me. And I do two things: if I'm standing up talking to them, I walk forward; if I'm sitting down, I get up, and it's almost a physical thing of drawing them up out of their chairs. And I do move around the outside. It's almost like pushing them in, into the melée. I suppose it's the same thing, you're encouraging them round the outside, not letting them escape.

H: Often I'll go into the middle of the group and create a focus which attracts them, and pulls them out of their sitting positions. But that was the first time I'd been so aware of the need to 'corral' a group. I felt like a sheep-dog.

J: So your intuitive response is an unconscious reaction to what's going on. Do you find that once you are working intuitively, you continue at that level? Or is it an isolated response to a particular event?

H: Certainly with that group, the feeling that something was wrong was so intense that I guess I switched over to 'intuitive mode'. It wasn't a normal situation, and so my normal ways of working weren't going to be effective. I think the 'corralling' thing was the beginning of that. I must have decided to trust to my feelings on this one. I had to. I didn't consciously know what to do. Literally every ten minutes, for example, throughout the morning, somebody got up to go to the toilet. I was leading the afternoon session and I spent a lot of time, over lunch, thinking about how to tackle that behaviour. It felt like such a deliberately disruptive act — a statement that they were making as a group about themselves and their attitudes. I felt that I had to completely change the atmosphere and show them that it was possible to shift the dynamics within the team. I felt that I had to indicate that I knew how bad things were. But I didn't know how to do it. I had a few ideas, but I wasn't really sure what to do. I wasn't until I was back in the room, confronted by the group, that I felt fully engaged with the problem. I hadn't worked out what to do or say, and I was standing in front of them; without thinking, purely on instinct, I said:

> 'I'm going to give you some feedback. I found the morning very difficult. I felt you weren't listening very clearly to the instructions we were giving. I felt you weren't listening to each other. You say that you want to improve communications within the team, and I can see why. I can see why you've got communication problems, just by how you've been in the morning. What I want to do now is tackle that head-on. I'm going to ask you to do an activity which I hope will encourage you to listen to each other. Ok? That will last for an hour and a half, and then I'm going to break and give you a chance to have a cup of tea and go to the toilet. What I'm going to ask of you is that you don't go to the toilet before then. Ok?'

I was quite hard, not angry or aggressive but very assertive in the delivery. And then at the end of it, I said: 'And I want to go to the toilet too, so I know how it feels!'. I don't know where that came from, I don't know why I said it, I really don't!

J: But it released them.

H: It released them. And it forced them to see me as a human being. Whereas before they were turning the trainer into someone to resist. They were using the trainer as an outlet for their frustration. And I came along and said, first 'I'm not putting up with that,' and second 'I'm vulnerable, I'm human, you can't turn me into a baddy!'. That was the beginning of the process of turning them round. It made what came next possible, I think. I asked them to do 'rounds' where each person had two minutes to speak about the area of difficulty they were having in communication. I put them into three groups of six and said to them: 'Don't interrupt the person who is talking. Don't answer them back when they've finished. Just go on to the next person'. And the atmosphere shifted, just like that. Quite radically, the whole atmosphere in the room changed. Nobody went to the toilet until we broke for tea!

J: So is there a general principle there or advice that somebody could pick up?

H: I think there are a number of things. First, I had to sort out my own feelings and be clear about what I wanted out of the situation.

What I was feeling in the morning was: 'I don't want to be here. I really don't want to be involved in this'. I was beginning to resent them for it! I had to struggle to stay separate, and recognise that they weren't behaving like that because of me, or because of my material. Second, I trusted to my instinct to deal with the situation. I didn't make any conscious decisions. I struggled with my feelings over lunch, struggled to stay positive, really. But when I stood up to speak, I hadn't worked out what I was going to say, nor in any detail what I was going to do. And it turned out that I was committed to the situation, and I was committed to the group, and I was taking responsibility for my part in what happened. My part was that I had the power and the experience to change the situation. So, third, I declared my power. It comes back to power and authority, I felt that what I did, intuitively, was be absolutely clear that I had power in the situation, and that I was going to use that power for the benefit of the group.

J: The other principle that seems to shout out at me is that if you do take that kind of approach, you've got to bring it back full circle, you've got to think about releasing people from the new tension that you've held them in. Having declared your power, you needed to mitigate it in some way to stop it being oppressive. You needed to give them back some power in the situation.

H: Having done the 'round', I gave them some areas of choice about how we proceeded for the rest of the afternoon. That was my way of doing that, of re-empowering them. That was intuitive, too. I hadn't planned to do that. It came to me without thinking.

J: I don't always feel, intuitively, that I can get away with that kind of direct challenge. There are situations when it's just too unequal to try and take a group on in that way — if I'm working with the entire staff of a school, for example. But I have done it with groups of teachers from different areas or schools. And I've certainly done it on residential courses when we've struggled through to the end of the day and there's something wrong or it's really hard work because of reactions, hostility, resentment, or just playing around, just not taking it seriously. I've gone to bed and not been able to sleep because it's all been going round and round in my head and then many, many times I've had a flash of inspiration about what to do in the morning. Sometimes it's been facing them with it, giving them feedback about how I've felt and where I've thought we'd got to yesterday. Or sometimes it's been a complete change of plan of what we were going to do. There have been many times when I've got up the next morning and I've had a new insight and I don't know where that comes from, just turning it over and over in my mind — its almost like I can't get to sleep until it's sorted.

H: I'm much more intuitive now than when I started training. I use my intuition more. I feel more confident that it will deliver the goods. It doesn't always. But it does most of the time now. I have no idea of how it developed, though. I don't think I consciously developed my intuition. But I'm not sure if it's just a matter of experience, and the confidence that grows with experience.

J: I think people's intuitive skills can develop as they become more experienced as a trainer. But they don't automatically. They have to be open to their own development. One of the problems, I think, is if trainers don't see themselves as needing to develop, continually, and don't use each experience they have as a trainer as an opportunity to develop. There have been times when I've been aware of a voice inside me which is nudging me somehow, either drawing my attention to something, or suggesting I do something. But often I only become aware of it after the event, and usually when I've ignored or suppressed it. So I'll think 'I wish I'd done so and so,' or 'I wish I'd said that,' you know. And the voice will say, 'Well, I told you to, it's your own fault,' do you know what I mean? And that's one of the ways I've become aware of my intuitive responses. Now I try to listen to those voices clearly, and respect them. Because more often than not they're right.

H: So what you are saying is that you try to monitor your feelings, to be aware of their promptings, and to trust those promptings?

J: Yes. Especially with reading the situation. My skill in that has grown as I've gone along, the more I'm faced with situations to read. I think I've built up a reservoir of experience, which I tap into. Getting feedback from co-trainers has been very important. It has helped me to recognise and use those experiences, to store them away and draw on them. And that's not about technique. It's different from developing technically as a trainer. You are developing your instinct. There's an exercise I do when I'm training trainers which is one of the ways I draw attention to it. It's a warm-up really, where we all sit round, and I say things like: 'Change seats if you think you're good at designing programmes,' and some change and some don't. Or: 'Change seats if you like leading best; change seats if you like supporting best'. And one of the categories is, 'Change seats if you think you're good at reading situations'. Somehow people know what that means, trainers who are learning to train, and some get up and some don't, and I always go back to them and say, 'Would anyone like to say why they didn't get up for that?'. I use it as a warm-up, but there's an awful lot in that exercise.

H: Does it lead on to discussion about using instinct? Is that a concern for them?

J: We deal with the importance of being observant, alert and perceptive. They accept that. But, inevitably I suppose, it moves on to 'What do you do about it?'. Their concern is far more about responding to situations which they haven't planned for. Or improvising when they see that what they've planned is inappropriate. And that's true for me, too. That's when I have sleepless nights, worrying about what to do with a particular group. When I have to go in the next morning and say: 'What I planned to do this session won't work, because I think there are some things we need to sort out first'. But I find that trainers, particularly those who are just starting out, find it very difficult to do that. They are operating on so many levels. They are trying to learn to read situations and needs. They may be learning to work together as trainers. The plan, the programme they have designed, becomes the main thing, and they are very reluctant to let go of it.

H: A clear structure for the day does provide a lot of security. You have to be very confident to be flexible, to take the risk of dropping everything and making it up as you go along.

J: The trouble is that a rigid adherence to a plan or a technique can make things very mechanical. You lose warmth and spontaneity. It turns people off, I think. It's a long process, though, developing flexibility and being confident enough to see what happens. I still like to plan meticulously, but know that I've got a number of options, and be ready to change in a flash. And I've got the confidence to do it, to say: 'I don't think what we were going to do is right,' and we'll work out something else.

H: But it is, then, giving a primacy to intuition, isn't it, and saying: 'In this situation, I need to work intuitively'?

J: One of the worries people have is that it may involve dropping the original objectives of the course, at least for a while. The official objectives, if you like. But there are times when you have to do that, because the official objectives won't be achieved until you sort out what's going on. Like your example just now. There's no point ploughing on mechanically if the dynamic within the group is problematic, and is dominating what's going on. So I think you always need to be aware of your instincts, and be ready to switch into 'intuitive mode' when the situation demands.

H: It feels dangerous, though, to say, 'The basis of effective training is instinct', because that feels so flimsy, such an insubstantial thing to say. A lot of trainers seem more interested in developing a theory or rationale for their work, or in making their work fit some superordinate ideology that they have. And I tell them that it's more important that they develop their intuition. I don't feel comfortable saying it, mainly because I think it's hard for them to use such advice. But it's what I've come to believe, in the end.

J: But we are not saying to trainers, '*Don't* try and establish a rationale for your work'. We are not saying, 'You *only* need to develop your intuition'.

H: I think rationale is not that useful for trainers, though. Especially if it gets in the way of them being flexible in response to the group. To me it comes down to whether you're working in the interests of the people you are training with, or in the interests of the ideology that you serve. I think it has to be the former.

J: Which is not to say that trainers should be blanks, with no rationale or value-system to call their own. Nor that they shouldn't be clear about what their values are if the situation requires it.

H: Absolutely. But there have been times when I have participated, as a learner, in other people's sessions, and I've felt that they have had a clear rationale for what they're doing, and that if I don't conform, as a learner, to their theory of how I should learn, then that's my fault. I've felt that they were quite inflexible in response to me, in real terms, even though they have appeared to be flexible in the way they have run the day. As if they were being flexible because they knew that's what they should be, but they weren't being really responsive. And other learners were getting irritated and confused. I'm thinking of one particular incident here, and it's because there was this strange feeling that the trainers were doing their thing, and we were like bit players in the show. I felt they were so determined to do things according to their book that they lost sight of us and our needs completely. I ended up feeling manipulated and resentful.

J: So their rationale made them self-conscious about how they actually behaved as trainers? That's what I mean about people becoming mechanical. It's to do with not being responsive to what's happening in the present. An example of that is this business of reflecting questions back on to the learner. If they ask a question, you reply by asking it back to them, you know! Well that's very much a technique born out of a rationale. And most of the time that's sound, when you genuinely want to know what they think, or when it's important that they find the answers for themselves. But I've seen trainers do it all the time, as a fixed response. In the end, people get really irritated with it. I've seen somebody ask a question and then add quickly, 'And don't you bloody well turn it back to me! I want to know what you think!'. That's why intuition is so much more important than ideology: it tells you whether the techniques are appropriate in any one situation. And they are not always appropriate.

H: Exactly! They were doing that, turning things back onto the group in this session I was talking about. But it wasn't working, because what people were asking was: 'What are the objectives of the session?'. They needed some clarity about what the purpose was. And the trainers wouldn't say, but kept asking it back: 'Well, what do you want out of the session?'. On one level that's fair enough. But I would have sorted that out right at the beginning. I would have enabled people to identify their expectations, and I would have been clear about what my objectives were, and taken it from there. But because they didn't do that, and were turning any questions back onto the questioner, people ended up feeling confused and suspicious. Not because they weren't prepared to think it out for themselves, but because the trainers seemed so patronising. It felt like we were being made to jump through hoops. The session was about self-managed learning, and they were clearly trying to model what self-managed learning was. But in the end I felt that what they wanted was for me to come away from the day agreeing with them, taking on their beliefs. I felt imposed on by them, actually. And my fantasy is that they'd see that as my fault, as me being resistant. Maybe I was . . .

J: But it's not good enough for trainers to say: 'I was OK, but that lot, God they were so resistant, I couldn't do anything with them!'. It's the trainer's responsibility to deal with people's resistance, and help them overcome it. It may not be the trainer's responsibility that people are resistant in the first place, but it's absolutely their responsibility to do something about it. That's one of the problems with people who are adhering to a strict rationale for their work. They end up protecting the rationale from the inconsistencies of real live people. They generate resistance in people, and then blame them for being resistant. It comes back to what you said: it comes back to whether they are working for the people in front of them or the ideology behind them.

H: I certainly came away from that day feeling that rationale is dangerous because it is likely to restrict intuition. If a trainer is too heavily focused on being consistent with a rationale which governs their work, I believe they will be less effective, because they will be less responsive to people, less able to respond. They will be working too much from their heads. They won't be working from their feelings. They'll probably be suppressing any of their own feelings if they contradict their rationale, come to think of it. I know for me, looking back, that the work I'm most pleased with has been when I'm working from my instinct or intuition. I'm at my best then. I feel in touch with what's going on. I feel more alive to it. I'm basically a lot more effective.

Summary

Although we never finally agreed on the semantic distinctions between instinct and intuition, we do agree that they contribute significantly in three areas. As trainers, we feel that we use them to:

- read the situation — to become aware of the nature of a group, to sense its needs, and to understand the dynamics between sub-groups or individuals;
- formulate responses — intuitive responses to certain situations are generated, often unconsciously, and especially in extreme or difficult circumstances;
- time the delivery of responses or interventions — feeling out the right time to suggest an activity or change of pace, or to challenge a group or intervene between individuals.

Instinct and intuition become particularly crucial if the trainer is not retaining the power in the learning situation. Timing the shift of power towards the group requires an instinctive understanding of when people are receptive to such initiatives. Knowing when and how to exert your authority for the welfare of the group also requires an intuitive feel for defining the problem and deciding appropriate action.

Instinct and intuition are not tangible skills that the trainer can learn and practise. They are ways of understanding and responding to the behaviour of groups and individuals. In part, they develop with experience, alongside the confidence to depart from the planned when confronted with the unexpected. In part they are always there, a voice inside you that warns and advises. Often that voice is only acknowledged in retrospect, after it has been ignored or suppressed. Trusting your instinct and intuition, listening to the inner voice, is the best way of developing its availability for you as a trainer.

We believe that if a trainer encourages their instinct and intuition to develop, they become more flexible. They become more able to respond to the hidden agendas of a learning group, to the inter-personal dynamics and the personal problems. They become less rigidly attached to the programme that has been planned, more able to improvise if necessary, to work intuitively. They become focused on the people they are working with, and on what is happening to those people in the present. They become less focused on themselves, on their technique, on the rationale which governs their technique. They become less rigid, and more open.

Activity

Below are a series of questions which you may wish to use to reflect on your responses to the issues we have discussed in this chapter, and the ways in which they relate to your experience as a trainer.

1 We feel that there is a tendency for trainers to repress their instinct or intuition for fear that it will be disruptive of what has been planned. Do you feel that you tend to listen to or ignore your instinct or intuition when you are operating as a trainer?

2 We strongly advocate the use of instinct and intuition in training. Do you agree with us? Or do you feel that the use of such qualities is irrelevant, or worse, to the training process?

3 We suggest that a trainer's development is partly a process of developing their instinct and intuition so that they become more flexible and more responsive. Do you agree with this? Or do you feel that such qualities are irrelevant to a trainer's development?

4 We believe that there is sometimes a conflict between instinct/ intuition and an adherence to technique or particular training philosophy or dogma. Are you aware of this conflict, either in yourself, or in other trainers that you have seen working? If so, do you feel, as we do, that such adherence can restrict instinct

and intuition, and so make the trainer less able to respond to the immediate needs of the people they train?

Comment

Our emphasis on the value of instinct and intuition reflects the kind of training that we have both been involved in. It also reflects the objectives that we have brought to our work, objectives which include the possibility of personal as well as professional development.

Trainers who work in areas of practical skills development may see less value in such qualities. They may seem irrelevant to the clearly-defined situations in which they work. Trainers who work in areas of interpersonal skills development may be more aware of their use of intuition or instinct, and feel that they are a necessary part of their repertoire.

Although the degree of utility may vary depending on context, we believe that instinct and intuition are important attributes for all trainers, and, for that matter, for people-workers of all kinds. We are also aware that the words mean different things to different people: a private sector trainer we spoke to referred to his 'gut-feel', and how he felt happiest when he was working from his gut! He also said that there were periods when it abandoned him, and he didn't know why, and then it would come back, and again, he didn't know why. He wanted to know how he could have more control over his gut-feel, whilst at the same time recognising that if it was controllable it would probably lose its power and effectiveness. In the end we agreed that the secret was not to try and control it, but to let it control you, and wished we could say something that was a bit more practical!

3 Responsibility

In the introduction we stated that one of the principles of active learning is to share responsibility for learning with the learner. This raises questions about the nature of the trainer's responsibility. On the surface it would seem to conflict with a philosophy in which we also both believe, expressed neatly by Keith Johnstone in his book *Impro*:

> Many teachers don't seem to think that manipulating a group is their responsibility at all. If they're working with a bored group, they blame the students for being 'dull' or uninterested. It's essential for the teacher to blame himself if the group aren't in a good state.

This chapter focuses on this dilemma: where does the responsibility of the trainer end and that of the learner begin? We explore our understanding of where our responsibility as trainers lies. If we are handing over responsibility for learning to the learner, what is it that we are responsible for?

J: I believe that the trainer starts out holding much of the responsibility for what is going to happen on a course. At the beginning they are responsible for any development, personal or professional, that is going to take place. But they need to be continuously looking for ways of encouraging the group to take on that responsibility for themselves. The learner won't develop significantly unless they have taken responsibility for their own development. If this doesn't happen, there will still be a dependence on the trainer which will get in the way of them continuing their development after the course, when the trainer is not there. The trainer needs to find ways of sharing responsibility with the group, and of letting the group know that that is what they will be trying to do. Most 'turbulence' on a course comes about because of the learner's unwillingness to take responsibility for their own learning.

H: I think that it is difficult for trainers to let go of those feelings of responsibility. It's difficult for me not to see the group as a reflection of me and my ability as a trainer. I have to stay separate from a group, keep an emotional distance from them, in order not to get entangled in this way. If I have too great an investment in people changing, it creates a dynamic where they are doing it for me, as opposed to doing it for themselves. If the trainer doesn't stay separate, their investment in the success of the course can put a pressure on the learner which is not a healthy motivation. It actively works against the learner taking responsibility for themselves. It becomes a very parental relationship.

J: You have to prevent that relationship from developing. It clouds the issue so much. It gets in the way. Handing over responsibility to the learner is not irresponsible. It's a very sophisticated process, I think. It's about developing the autonomy of the learner. The trainer's responsibility lies in managing that handover, and in creating the environment where it can take place.

H: I think the problem stems from a misunderstanding about what being 'caring' is. I once observed a trainer I felt was trying to be — the only way I can describe it is — the 'mummy' of the group. She was caring for them in a way that was inappropriate to the training situation. It was too much. She would take on too much responsibility for them getting it right. And when they didn't, she got angry with them for failing her. The group were confused about the kind of relationship she was trying to establish. On the one hand she was this mummy/carer, and on the other hand she was their trainer/authority figure. So they ended up playing naughty children to her mummy, basically. And she got into all sorts of difficulties. I think that it is often counter-productive to get too close to the group. It's wise to keep a distance. Which is not to say that you have to hold yourself aloof from them. I will set out to generate warmth, often through using physical contact, for example. But I want to be clear that I'm not one of them, I'm the trainer. I have a job to do. I don't want to confuse people that I'm anything else.

J: When I'm training people, I'm there to serve them. My needs, my life, my background, are out of the frame. If they start asking me about myself, during informal sessions in the bar or whenever, I minimise the amount I tell them in order to continuously put them back in the frame. I tell them enough about myself to satisfy them and for them to feel that I am a real person, and that's all. When I'm training, I forget myself. I put myself into their frame of reference and maintain that frame all the time. A group tends to see me as a very powerful person, inevitably, because I'm 'the trainer'. I am in a very powerful position. If I chose to, I could dominate the available space. I could easily become the most important person in the room. One of the factors in handing over responsibility is this process of staying out of the frame as much as possible, and putting them in it.

H: There is a strange invisibility to it all sometimes. I remember talking to a man one evening about how he was feeling about the course. I knew that he was worried about doing roleplays and we'd used roleplay activities that day. He was saying that he still didn't like them, but he'd joined in because he felt the group was so supportive; yes, he had got a lot out of the activities, but only because of the people in the group. I realised that he must have had experiences of roleplay in high-risk situations, or on courses where the group had not been bonded beforehand. But he didn't see the difference in terms of how this course had been run, or in the fact that we weren't irresponsibly shoving things at him. It was to do with the people on the course.

J: That often happens to me. People will put the success of a course down to the people there. They'll say: 'Oh well, it wouldn't be the same with another group, this was a special group,' and so on. They don't recognise that the course has been managed so that it generates the support and generosity and feelings of accomplishment that they feel so good about at the end.

H: I get caught by that. There's part of me that wants the recognition for having been instrumental in developing the climate of the course. But I also find it quite flattering that they are unaware of what I have done. Because it means that they feel responsible for the success of the course, and I'd rather they felt good about themselves than good about me. I know that in my head, but I still want the recognition!

J: One of the major pieces of learning that I've had as a trainer is learning what a lonely place it is. If you've developed a sense of achievement for the group, and for the individuals within the group, for the duration of a course, they'll go off at the end feeling great, and really warm towards each other. And you're left there high and dry. It took me a long time to accept that place. I wanted some acknowledgement, some of the warmth. I've had to come to terms with it. And I do it by saying to myself: 'Well, I've done my job well. If that's how it is at the end, I've done my job well'.

H: It is a natural outcome of believing that it is important for the learner to be responsible for their own learning. Do you ever draw the learner's attention to the fact that you want to share responsibility in the situation? Do you let them know overtly that that's what you want to happen?

J: The only time that I spell it out is in my introductory remarks at the beginning of the course. I'll say something like: 'On this course responsibility for learning will be shared. That's not just an idle phrase. From time to time we shall be thinking about where the responsibility is located, and how much responsibility we are each taking, not just for ourselves, but for other people as well. So that if somebody is expressing a need or a misunderstanding, or is feeling disturbed, the automatic reaction shouldn't be: "Well, she'll take care of that, she's the trainer, it's nothing to do with me," — it's got to be to do with us all'. I also say: 'Now that's probably gone in one ear and out the other'. And it usually has! It's a difficult concept to internalise. People won't respond just to me telling them that's what's going to happen. It's a process. Sometimes it happens quickly. Occasionally it seems as if it's never going to happen. But it's my responsibility to make sure that it does happen.

H: Are there signs that you can recognise as being key points in the process of them taking responsibility?

J: It's more to do with the experiences they have on the course. The activities I use are designed specifically to encourage the learner to take responsibility for their own learning. There is a central activity on our courses which is the key point of challenge for the learner. It is a task where the participants have to put into practice what they have learnt so far on the course. They have to plan how to carry out the task, and they have to carry it out in a real-life situation. And they have to choose whether to meet the challenge. I help them prepare, and we structure feedback, but the doing of it is up to them.

H: Isn't that a very high-risk strategy? What happens if they won't do it, or don't feel able to do it?

J: It is high-risk. But it is often the turning point in terms of responsibility. There was one course where we were training a group of very inexperienced trainers. The task we had designed for them to

do, on the second day, was to run a course for other people. I told
them this in a pre-course meeting and nobody even blinked. I knew
that they were thinking: 'Well she's saying that, but she'll be the
one who steers us through. She'll take responsibility for it'. And
all through the first day, it was incredibly difficult to get them to
come up with suggestions about what they were going to do, and
to make decisions about who would do what bits, and how everybody could make a contribution. By the evening session we just
hadn't got anywhere with them! So the other trainer and I agreed
that we were just going to go back after dinner and say nothing,
which was something we'd never done before, a real encounter
group strategy! And they clowned around and waited for the
session to start and we just sat there, silent. It must have taken
about forty-five minutes before somebody said: 'Well the time's
running out and we still haven't decided what we're going to do
tomorrow,' and we sat there, and said nothing, and gradually they
started working. It was a terrific risk, because they could have felt
like we were playing games with them, and rejected the whole
thing. The truth was that we were desperate, we didn't know what
else to do. I suppose we'd have had to take responsibility if it
hadn't come off, because we couldn't mess around the people that
we'd arranged to come in on the second day. But in the end it went
really well. They did it all themselves, and didn't look to us to bail
them out at all. And at the de-briefing session afterwards, it was
clear that the learning that came out of it for them was profound.
They had got a huge amount out of it.

H: Did they think that they had?

J: They all felt that they'd made a hash of it, initially. We had to take
back some responsibility to get them to see for themselves how far
they'd developed as trainers, so that they could go away the following morning with a sense of achievement. Which they did.

H: If you hadn't taken back the responsibility at the end, do you think
they wouldn't have been able to learn from the experience? Would
they have sabotaged it through their insecurity, is that what you
mean?

J: What they were saying about it was generally negative. It was as if
they wanted us to confirm that it was negative. There was certainly
no way that they were going to let in our feedback about how well
they had done. So taking back the responsibility didn't mean us
telling them anything in that sense. But we had to enable them to
get to the end of the course recognising that they had moved on, so

that they went away believing that they could do it again in other situations. We were directive about how we did that. We set up exercises where they gave each other feedback, and we got them to make their remarks fit into a particular framework. So, for example, we would say: 'The next thing I want you to do is give your partner one piece of negative feedback, just one, something that you feel they didn't do well, or you didn't agree with, or you thought they could have done better. Now do it — go on'. We were very authoritarian. And they did it, and then the opposite, 'Now give them a piece of good feedback, something they did well'. Then we did a round about how they felt about the whole experience and their own contribution to it. And, almost without exception, they were positive.

H: If, at the end of that kind of process, somebody continues to feel negative about themselves or what they did, do you see it as your responsibility to shift them into the positive. If, say, somebody in that final round, because of their low self-esteem, or for whatever personal reason, was insisting on maintaining a negative position, what would you do?

J: I think I would recognise that I couldn't do any more than I had. I suppose I would have felt responsible, but there would be absolutely nothing I could have done about it. They were all going off home, and we were catching a train back to Lancaster. I've learned to come to terms with that. I'm a fairly pragmatic person. What can't be done can't be done.

H: There are times when I have felt it as a failure on my part if somebody doesn't shift. There was a woman on a course I ran, who at the end of it, despite a lot of input and a lot of support, was determined to feel bad about herself. She made it quite clear that she was feeling bad about herself. And I was very upset. I felt responsible. I felt concerned for her. They had been a difficult group. They had been very reluctant to take any responsibility, and she had been particularly difficult, especially on the first day. But she came up to me at the beginning of the second day, and said that she felt very bad about how she'd been the day before, and she apologised to me, which I thought was very courageous of her. We had set up that on the second day they each had to run a short training session for the other course members. She said she had been very worried about doing this. I knew she had been, and thought she was going to tell me that she wasn't going to do it. But she told me that she'd decided what she was going to do in that

session and asked me what I thought about it. I was very positive,
genuinely. I was pleased she had decided to do it, and I thought
her choice of topic was excellent and that the way she was planning
to do it seemed fine. I decided that I wouldn't give her too much
input, but let her take off on her own from the position she'd
started the day with. Maybe that was a mistake. Because the
reverse happened. She sabotaged her own session. It was going
fine until she sabotaged it. She threw her notes down and walked
out. The rest of the group were very supportive of her, very
reassuring. But she refused to let it in. I felt there was a lot going
on for her in that situation which meant that there was no way that
she could allow herself to be successful. I really felt for her, and
the power of what was going on for her there. But there was
nothing I could do. I felt that I'd created a situation which was
very hurtful for her.

J: I think that the most important thing for her is that she started to
get the support of the group. She can continue to meet with them,
in a way that she can't with you. Maybe she was using that session
as an opportunity of alerting the group to her need for support.
I can think of one or two people like the one you've described.
And they have continued to meet with the group. The very fact
that the person feels wanted and included has effectively changed
their view of themselves. They haven't been able to persist with
their negative feelings about themselves. And I know that there's
nothing I can do about it anyway, so there's no point in worrying.
I suppose you could keep in touch with them somehow, but you
would be doing that more for yourself than for them, to reassure
yourself that it's not that bad. I tend to rely on the dynamic of the
group, which has been deliberately created through the course, to
do that for me.

H: I felt that I'd failed to create a sufficiently supportive dynamic
with that group. They all knew each other well. They had worked
together for years. But they weren't cohesive. And it was a two-
day course. The existing dynamic was so firmly established, that I
didn't think there was anything I could do about it. The course
had some effect on them, but I felt by the end that it was just a
drop in the ocean.

J: I think it is much harder to break the normative controls of a
group who work together or know each other, even if they can see
that they need to change. It's as though they can't do it from the
inside, and they'll look for something from the outside to effect a

change in the nature of the group. They will often use a trainer in that capacity. My experience is that when there's a group of people displaying certain types of behaviour, it's incredibly difficult to tackle that or effect change in any permanent way. I don't feel that it's my responsibility to take that on. The trouble is, though, that unless it's tackled, they might as well not be on the course, because it will obstruct things so badly. So I suppose there is a sense where it is my responsibility to help them with that dynamic in order to create a climate conducive to learning. If you ignore what's going on, it will continue to get in your way. But the responsibility there only lasts for the duration of the course. It's arrogant to believe that you can do any more than that. Irresponsible even!

H: I accept that. I think I am arrogant in that way sometimes. Set myself ridiculous objectives and then castigate myself for not achieving them. But in those situations, it's not just about not ignoring the problem. You can also 'enter' the problem. You could decide to approach it in quite a structured way, looking at it from outside, which wouldn't be ignoring it. But when you enter it, you use their problem as the learning material — the material that is to be focused on, that they are to learn from. And the learning that takes place is that you have to take responsibility for yourself, for your contribution to the problem. I've done that with groups before. But I failed with this one. I failed to get them to realise the need to take responsibility, and not just realise it, but feel it, for themselves. I failed because I stayed on the outside of the problem, looking in. I had to enter it, and take it head on. But I felt there wasn't the time to do that. And I felt that the problems were too entrenched for me to deal with. That it wouldn't have been responsible for me to try, and I got confused about where my real responsibility lay. When you enter the problem like that it becomes almost a form of group therapy. It feels like I'm entering a new zone, a new dimension, and I always feel nervous at that point. There are times when I won't do it. And this was one of them. But the effect was that I don't think it was a very effective course.

J: I think that kind of thing is what frightens people about a groupwork approach to training. The unpredictability of it, and wondering whether you'd be able to handle it, either as a group member or as a group leader. It's one of the reasons that I try to be as reassuring as possible, all the time, to whoever I'm working with, by saying: 'You take steps that you think you're ready for'. It's not enough to say that groups tend to look after themselves, that the level of disclosure is usually one that people feel comfortable with. They won't accept that, in the abstract. So I tend to reassure them from the beginning that they won't be led into areas that they don't want to go into, and they can control it for themselves by taking their own cautious steps.

H: I think I failed to do that. But I also felt that a lot of learning did take place on that course. I felt that the woman I talked about had learned an awful lot about herself. But it was unpleasant. Any learning experience is likely to be disturbing to people, at some level, because it's getting them to look at themselves and their behaviour. And for some people that may be a profoundly disturbing experience. I often get asked this when I'm training trainers. They worry about the extent of their responsibility for the learners. I say that if people are disturbed, it is an indication of the extent of learning taking place. You can't take responsibility for what people do with that learning. You have to see it as their responsibility and not get caught up in the disturbance. But I know from that woman how difficult it can be to stay separate, to resist getting caught up in it.

J: Which isn't to say that the trainer doesn't take on an awful lot of responsibility. I've worked hard at being observant, looking for signs all the time that somebody might be uncomfortable or disturbed. I won't always intervene. It depends on the degree of disturbance. But it's my responsibility to be aware of what's going on, and to evaluate whether there is a need for intervention. There's a contradiction there really: I work very hard to get people to take responsibility for their own learning and that of other people, and for supporting one another so that they share responsibility as a group. But for the time that we're together, I also take ultimate responsibility for the welfare of the group, and I work very hard to give them the reassurance that it's always there.

H: If you retain responsibility for the welfare of the group though, isn't there a danger that you create the parental relationship we were talking about before? Given that the process of sharing responsibility for learning is liable to generate disturbance and to upset people.

J: I think what I'm saying is that if we are to share responsibility, I have to force them to take their share. I don't relinquish my share. It's there all the time. So there isn't any distinction between welfare and learning. I don't think that they can be separated. They are too bound up together. The end goal for me is for people to recognise and absorb into themselves that we are ultimately responsible for our own actions. If somebody is disturbed by something that happens on a course, and it results in other, more painful experiences, if they persist in saying: 'This is all because of that course I went on', then I would feel that I'd failed. Not because I'd upset their lives. I'd failed because they were still saying that it was my fault. That's what I mean. I'd failed because they were still laying the responsibility on me, and because they were still avoiding taking responsibility for themselves.

Summary

In this chapter, we have looked at the dual nature of responsibility in active learning. The intention is for the learner to share responsibility for their own learning. But this doesn't happen automatically, nor on request. It is the trainer's responsibility to ensure that it happens, and this is one of the key responsibilities that the trainer holds during a course.

The learner is encouraged to take responsibility so that their learning is theirs, owned and controlled by the learner themselves. Success for the trainer is the achievement of this shared responsibility, and ultimately of the independence of the learner. This is more important than the learner performing to a standard seen as necessary by the trainer. Over-identifying with the group in this way will generally impede the independence of the learner. The difference is that they will perform according to the trainer's criteria, as opposed to being empowered to develop their own.

Likewise the trainer has to accept the risk that sharing responsibility can bring turbulence: feelings of resistance, hostility or disturbance. The trainer needs to stay separate, and not see turbulence as a reflection on their ability. Over-caring for the group can result in a confusing and symbiotic relationship which restricts the potential for the group to look after itself — to take responsibility for itself.

The successful development of autonomy often goes unnoticed by the group, who, at the end of a course, will be more focused on their own potency and achievement. The degree of recognition given to the trainer is often disproportionate to the amount of responsibility taken and energy given out. Looking to the group for recognition is inappropriate. But recognition is still needed if the trainer is to sustain their own motivation and energy.

Activity

Below are a series of questions which you can use to reflect on your responses to the issues we have discussed in this chapter, and the ways in which they relate to your experience as a trainer.

- *Having read the chapter, how do you divide up responsibility for learning in your work?*
  What do you see the trainer being responsible for?
  What do you see the learner being responsible for?
- *If you are concerned to share responsibility for learning with the learners, what indicators do you look for to gauge the degree to which they are taking responsibility during a course?*
- *How 'separate' are you from the participants on your courses?*
  Do you get very close to them, either on an equal level, or in a more 'professional' caring way?
  Do you keep your distance?
- *How do you tend to react if someone on a course becomes upset or disturbed as a result of the course?*
  Do you see it as your fault?
  Do you see it as your responsibility to resolve the feelings?
  Do you involve the rest of the group as support for the individual?

Comment

The answers to all these questions will depend very much on the kind of training you are involved in, and the objectives you set for your work. You may or may not agree that the autonomy of the learner is a key objective, for example, and this will radically affect your responses to this chapter.

Judging how best to intervene if someone becomes upset depends on the nature of your relationship with them. If you are never going to see them again after the course, it may be that responsibility is best exercised by identifying sources of support from within the group. This has primarily been our experience, and we work from the beginning to develop a supportive climate within the group that can last beyond the limits of the course. In-house trainers may adopt a very different strategy, and see it as part of their responsibility to support individuals in an on-going way.

We feel that being clear about the nature and boundaries of your responsibility as a trainer, both to yourself and the groups you train, is an important aspect in development. Consistent messages, clearly expressed, allow the group to set appropriate expectations of you, and of each other.

Section Three: Training As Professional Development

1 Training in context

The overriding aim of our work as trainers is to help people in their professional development. We stress the word 'help' because people tend to develop professionally whether they receive training or not. Development occurs naturally through experience. It is easy for us to underestimate people's ability to learn from their experience and to manage their own development. It is also easy for us to overestimate the benefits that can be derived from training. Training is only one factor in professional development, and it is a limited one. From the learner's perspective, training is an interruption of their natural course of development — an interruption that may or may not be appropriate, and that may or may not be useful.

In this section we will be focusing on the contribution that training can make, and on ways of making that contribution more durable. In order to do that, we have had to question what we mean by professional development. In particular, we have had to explore our perception of the boundary between professional and personal development, and the different perceptions held by the people who come on our courses and by the people who send them.

Three perspectives

The trainer's perspective

We find it hard to make a distinction between professional and personal development for two reasons. First, the basis of the way we work is to encourage people to take responsibility for their own learning and therefore to take control over their own development. They may apply *what* they learn only in the professional areas of their lives, but the process of empowering the learner is essentially one of personal growth.

Second, the people we train do not work in isolation. They work in large organisations alongside many other people. For us, a key aspect of professional development involves individuals in learning about themselves in relation to their organisation and the people they work with. Development occurs through self-awareness and awareness of others. And development can be sustained beyond the training event by learning how to support and be supported by others. This process of sensitising the learner to themselves and to other people is again essentially one of personal growth.

These two processes are the foundation of our work. They are not necessarily declared goals, although the learners' attention is drawn to them as the course progresses. We are more likely to describe the goals of a course beforehand as being to review development to date, and to plan for future development. And we will be referring to professional development. But we believe that if people are to develop professionally, and to continue developing professionally, the primary need is to develop flexibility on a personal level.

The learner's perspective

We have learnt to be cautious in referring openly to personal development as a goal in our work. We have often been told by people that they would have resisted a course which was described in such language. When we ask people about their expectations at the beginning of a course, there is a frequently expressed concern that they will have to expose themselves in some way, open themselves up to the group, operate on a 'feeling' level. Few people feel comfortable with such a prospect.

Often the learner's expectations of training are unclear. It is unusual for people to have identified what they want to get out of a course before it starts. This is as true of people who have chosen to come onto the course as it is of people who have had no choice. When we ask people to clarify their goals on the morning of the first day, they tend to focus on the development of knowledge or skills which will be of immediate value on their return to work. They want to separate the professional from the personal, and to work solely in the dimension of professional development.

One of the main sources of resistance that we encounter on courses is this difference of perspective on the meaning of the word development. As the course progresses two things happen: people see that the risks involved in an active approach to learning are less threatening than they feared; and they understand the limitations in separating the personal and the professional. By the end of a course, hopefully, people perceive that the benefits to be gained by working on a personal level outweigh the risks that they have taken. In the short term, they receive strong feelings of accomplishment from their participation on the course. In the longer term they have developed a self-awareness and self-confidence which we believe to be the cornerstone of future development.

The client's perspective

As external trainers, most of our training is commissioned by a manager from within an organisation, whom we refer to as the client. It is unusual for the client to participate as a learner in a training programme; their involvement occurs in the planning of the programme. The initial consultation with the client is an important stage in itself. They tend to have expectations of the programme which are different again to those of the trainer and the participants. There is often a tension between these three perspectives which needs to be resolved in order to agree a set of realistic goals for the programme.

The client's expectations will depend on their position within the organisation, and their closeness to the learner group. They have to marry the need for benefits to the organisation with the needs of the learners as individuals. In general, clients are more focused on professional development. Their goal is for people to return from the training better able to do their jobs. In some instances, this may involve elements of personal development, particularly if the culture and efficiency of the organisation is dependent on co-operation or teamwork. Occasionally this is the most explicit need, when training is being used as a strategy for resolving difficulties or conflict.

We have found that clients' expectations of training are often unrealistic or over-ambitious. Uncovering the needs of the client during the consultation phase is crucial in ensuring that the potential for disappointment or disillusion after the training is minimised. Disappointment in the training, although uncomfortable, is less damaging than disappointment in the learners. We work with clients to clarify the distinction between personal and professional development, and to reach a balance between short- and long-term benefits. We also try, whenever possible, to involve clients in the training process, so that they can become aware of the different perspectives of the learners. Generating such awareness can itself be a significant contribution. At the least it enables the client to incorporate likely outcomes of the training into their own expectations.

In our case, then, there are three different perspectives on the nature of training that have to be accommodated in some way. This is not always the case. Trainers who work purely in the sphere of professional development may not have the need to reconcile the different expectations of clients and learners. The goals are implicit within the nature of the training, whether they be to increase knowledge or develop skills. A process of accommodation may just confuse a situation that is already clear.

When the learning goals actively incorporate a move into the sphere of personal development, a process of consultation, both with clients and learners, is in effect the beginning of the learning process. Identifying and clarifying your own objectives for a course involves taking some responsibility for your own learning, and for the learning of others. We invariably start the process of empowering and sensitising by engaging the learner in such a consultation.

The contribution of training

People don't stand still. They develop all the time. Professional development takes place without training, just as learning takes place without teaching. But if people don't have an opportunity to reflect on their experience, there is a danger that the learning they derive from it may have a haphazard and coincidental effect on their development. People require skills and resources if they are to manage their own development successfully. People have varying degrees of skill in reviewing and learning from their experience. But most people lack the resources in their professional lives to do so consistently and incrementally. The resources most needed, and generally most lacking, are time and support.

Training is a planned and managed intervention in a person's natural development. It provides a limited but intensive opportunity for reflection and learning. The particular contribution of training is to provide a structured opportunity for the participant to:

- meet other people, usually from a similar professional background, share experiences with them, and gain assurance from that sharing;

- review recent experience, take stock of existing skills, and set new personal goals;
- reaffirm existing ways of doing things and experiment with and practise different approaches;
- work with other people, learn from their experience, and learn about themselves in relation to others.

Such opportunities are not in themselves dependent on training. But a structured learning process will not only ensure that the opportunities are created and their potential realised, it will also put people in a better position to manage their own development. They will have a heightened awareness of the issues involved for them personally; and they will have more options, in terms of skills and methods, for dealing with those issues.

The limitations of training

Training is *only* an intervention in a person's course of development. The contribution it can make is inevitably limited. Within the context of a person's life, even just their working life, a one-week course is a mere pin-prick! Life goes on. In many cases the impact of a course diminishes rapidly. Back at work, the old pressures resume and it becomes increasingly difficult to sustain any movement or change under the dead weight of the familiar.

The significance of training to any one individual at a particular time will depend on three main factors:

1 Their previous learning experiences. Some people are used to a participative approach to learning, and expect to take responsibility for their own learning. Others are used to more conventional teaching, and are unwilling to move into a more active role. Others again have such negative experiences that they are resistant to any kind of training at all.

2 Their present state of mind. Professional development may be low on a person's priorities at the time of the training event. Other events, at work or outside of it, may be more pressing. People aren't always at their most open and committed when you want them to be!

3 The culture of their organisation. Attitudes to training vary radically in different organisations. Often there is a gap between

stated aims regarding personal and professional development and what happens in practice. People tend to be influenced by actions more than words!

These issues are outside the trainer's control. All that we can do is attempt to minimise the limitations and maximise the potential impact. Often the key time is during consultation with the clients. We have evolved a framework for negotiating training with clients which we use to clarify the correlation between desired outcomes, the strategies used to achieve them, and the time available for doing so. It can be represented as shown in Figure 1.

We use this framework to negotiate with clients for more realistic goals within the time available, or for more time in order to make their goals achievable. The framework helps us to explain to clients the importance that we give to the training process. The active learning process is not necessarily an appropriate method for meeting every desired outcome. It is sometimes more appropriate for us to use didactic teaching methods in order to effectively meet the goals of our client within the limited time available. The framework demonstrates to the client the range of possible options, and the implications of each of those options. And it allows us to be flexible in meeting their demands.

The framework also helps us to be realistic. The limitations of training are frustrating. The temptation is always to try to achieve more than is possible. To try to do in half a day what can only be usefully achieved in a day — what we *know* can only be achieved in a day! This is often because of the perceived need of having to justify the value of training, or of demonstrating efficacy in order to negotiate for more time to do it properly next time. Often it is because of our vanity as trainers: we tend to over-aspire because of our own need for feelings of accomplishment. Holding our aspiration in check is a constant struggle. The framework helps us to focus on the needs of the learner.

The role of the trainer

The trainer's role is to plan, organise, manage and follow up the training intervention. As we have shown in previous sections of the book, we think that the role is complex and difficult. There are a number of intrinsic tensions.

Figure 1 *

Aims of training →	1 Updating Awareness raising	2 Examining new concepts & principles	3 Acquiring new skills, insights & understanding	4 Application, to job of new learning Self-awareness. Further development desired
Time available for training and kinds of approach possible in the time ↓	/////	/////	/////	/////
1 Short session of 1–2 hours *Input followed by discussion.*	✓			
2 Half a day or one whole day *Illustrative material eg video; practical group tasks.*	✓	✓		
3 Two days with a follow up later *Simulated tasks with feedback. Assignments in work place. Support, reflection.*	✓	✓	✓	
4 Three blocks of two days or a residential block of 3–5 days *Practical tasks in real settings with immediate feedback, challenge, reflection, and support.*	✓	✓	✓	✓

* Based on information from Joyce, R and Showers, B 'Improving Inservice Training: the messages of research' in *Educational Leadership* Feb 1980, pp 379–384. Matrix devised by Dr Ray Bolam, University of Bristol, for an evaluation of the *Active Tutorial Work* project (Blackwell, 1982)

On the one hand we have to forget our own needs in order to focus on the needs and expectations of the learners. On the other hand we have to be self-aware, and open to opportunities for growth and self-development. We must provide structure and direction, but look out for and be able to respond to needs for different structuring or for new directions. We have to challenge the learner, to move them into unexplored areas, and also support them, bearing in mind a range of needs, not just the need to develop. We work with groups which develop their own distinct identity, and are also working with the individuals that make up that group to ensure that they are not subsumed by the emerging group identity. We have a set of beliefs and values about training which we share with clients and learners. But part of that set is not to impose our values on others. We are responsible for managing the learning situation, and we work to shift the locus of power so that people take responsibility for their own learning.

These tensions mean that we are in a constant state of flux, moving from one extreme to another in order to generate and be responsive to what is going on out there. We have expressed this flux in a series of continua which describe different aspects of trainer behaviour, and the corresponding aspects of learner behaviour. We see ourselves as a 'dot' moving continually backwards and forwards along each continuum, and jumping from one continuum to another as required.

The trainer moves between being:

    in the forefront   < -------- to being -------- >   in the background

The learner moves between being:

    passive   < -------- *to being* -------- >   *active*

the trainer moves between being:

directive		non-directive
making decisions	< -------- to being -------- >	enabling decisions
taking the lead		following

the learner moves between being:

dependent		*planning*
following	< -------- *to being* -------- >	*self-programming*
uncommitted		*committed*

the trainer moves between being:

protective		challenging
sheltering	< -------- to being -------- >	exposing
controlling		releasing

the learner moves between being:

cared for		*experimental*
secure	< -------- *to being* -------- >	*insecure*
cautious		*creative*

the trainer moves between being:

energetic		quiet
	< -------- to being -------- >	
forcing the pace		reflective

the learner moves between being:

observing rules		*leading*
un-reflective	< -------- *to being* -------- >	*pace-setting*
distanced		*involved*

the trainer moves between being:

judging		reviewing
	< -------- to being -------- >	
assessing		facilitating reflection

the learner moves between being:

assessed		*evaluating*
passive	< -------- *to being* -------- >	*self-programming*
dependent		*self-managing*

Both ends of each continuum describe behaviours which are necessary to the trainer's repertoire. Different places on the continua will be appropriate at different times during a training course. The temptation, for us, is to anchor ourselves somewhere near the right-hand end. The skill is to be able to move freely around the model.

At some stage on a course, the trainer will be located somewhere on each continuum. As shown in the model, their behaviour causes an effect in the learners' behaviour. For example, the trainer may start by being active, energetic and directive. The learners may start by being a passive audience, only mildly motivated. The trainer's aim may be to move along the various continua to a position of unobtrusive facilitator, with the learners managing their own learning. Along the way the trainer moves freely around the model, protecting some individuals, challenging others, providing energy when energy is flagging, taking a new direction if required, reviewing and facilitating reflection when appropriate.

Elements in the training process

The trainer's role is to manage the training process. The model above is a management model describing the behaviour options that can be chosen by the trainer at any one time in order to manage the process effectively. The training process requires skilful management if it is to contribute to professional and personal development. It also requires a structure if it is to enable people to continue to develop after the course is finished, when they are back in the eroding familiarity of their normal lives.

We have identified five elements to that structure which we believe are essential to training which promotes continuing development. These are:

1 *Climate*: the creation and maintenance of a climate which is reassuring and secure, which taps and releases energy, which promotes openness and sensitivity to others.

2 *Support*: the provision of opportunities to learn from others, and the promotion of a willingness to forget self in an atmosphere of encouragement and challenge.

3 *Stepping*: the overall shape of a course, involving a series of steps, each dependent on the previous one being completed, in an incremental development of challenge and support.

4 *Challenge*: the deepening of the quality of experience for the learners, moving into new areas of awareness, involving varying degrees of risk at different stages of a course.

5 *Reflection*: the evaluation of what has taken place during the course and its relation to life outside the course; reflection is a significant step towards continuing self-appraisal and development.

These elements are all present in different degrees throughout a course. They are continually overlapping, but the order they are listed in above describes a sequence in which the different elements come to the fore. In the following chapters of this section, we will explore each element in turn.

2 Creating a climate

We describe our work as being about professional development. We describe our courses in terms of skill and knowledge development. But we make no distinction between the personal and the professional. We don't divide people up into working and non-working selves. We regard our work as being about personal development.

We reconcile this apparent contradiction by giving equal value to the content of a course and the processes in which that content is imparted to the learner. We address the learner's professional needs in the content. We work on a personal level in the process. People coming on a course are generally more interested in *what* they are going to learn than in *how* they are going to learn. By involving them immediately in clarifying and sharing the *what*, we begin to involve them in the *how*. As the course progresses, the what and the how become increasingly interconnected, until by the end they are virtually indistinguishable.

This strategy of involving people in the learning process, giving them some measure of control over it, is often very disruptive. It is not what people are expecting. It can seem irrelevant. It can feel disturbing, even threatening. In order for it to work, we have to pay great attention to creating a climate within the learning group which will encourage and allow people to move beyond what they expected, to bear with the seeming incongruity, to take the risks. Climate, however, is not just important when active, participatory learning methods are being used. Effective learning is dependent on a conducive climate. Without such a climate, we believe that the quality and durability of learning is greatly reduced.

The existing climate

Climate governs how people feel about being on the course, which in turn governs the quality of learning that will take place. A climate exists before the course starts, made up of the hopes and anxieties, the energy and tension that people bring with them. This is affected by initial contact with other course members, by the reaction to the physical surroundings, the way the room has been arranged, and by the impression gained of the trainer as they prepare to start.

Our first task is to 'read' this existing climate in order to have some awareness of how people are feeling, and of how people are behaving towards each other. We are particularly attuned to the level of openness and trust that exists within the group, for this is the foundation on which we have to build. Our aim is to create a climate which is both open and supportive. For this to happen, people need to feel able to express themselves on a feeling level, and be receptive to the expression of the feelings of others. They need to feel able to share with others, and to be open to new insights and new self-awareness. They need to feel secure, and they need to feel able to use that security as a platform for meeting challenges and taking risks.

It is rare for us to find an existing climate which doesn't need modifying in some way. In most instances people are, quite rightly, wary of committing themselves. In some cases they are determined not to. In the initial stages of the course, most of our attention is given over to generating a climate which encourages people to drop their guard, to feel confidence in us, and to be aware of others. We need to monitor the climate constantly throughout the course because it changes and develops as the course progresses. But our responsibility for climate is greatest at the beginning. After the initial stages, we work to develop the group's awareness of the climate, and to encourage people to take some responsibility for it. It is in creating a climate for learning where we believe the trainer has to be most incisive and energetic. It is too important to be left to chance.

The components of climate

Climate is one of the key factors in moving learners to take responsibility for their own learning. A climate which is cold and uncomfortable is likely to be unproductive. A climate which is insecure and unsupportive is likely to be inhibiting. We attempt to modify the existing climate to create a learning environment which:

1 *Provides reassurance* Learners need an early indication of the nature of the involvement and contribution that is expected of them during the course. They need to feel that they will be able to learn and develop, and that what they have to offer will not be ignored or dismissed. They need the security of feeling that they can make mistakes without being ridiculed. And they need to know that other people share their hopes, fears and expectations.

2 *Releases energy* Learners may be unaware of their potential for development. They may expect to passively absorb knowledge and are unprepared for becoming energetically involved. On the other hand there may be an abundance of energy which is directed towards avoiding or resisting learning, or which is bound by normative controls that harness energy in unproductive ways. A climate needs to be established which releases people's energy, and which channels it outwards so that it contributes productively to the energy of the whole group.

3 *Engenders support* Awareness of other people's learning needs is an essential component of a climate which is conducive to learning. Being supported and encouraged by fellow learners builds confidence in the capacity to learn. Support does not preclude competitiveness or acknowledgement of failure. It encourages challenge, risk-taking and learning from mistakes.

4 *Generates motivation and commitment* Providing reassurance, releasing energy and engendering support help to generate motivation among individuals, and to establish their commitment to the group as a whole. Motivation and commitment are crucial to the maintenance of a healthy climate. They are also key indicators of the group's willingness to take risks and to evaluate their learning.

5 *Prepares for challenge* At the same time as providing reassurance, the climate needs to prepare people for the possibility of challenge. A balance needs to be struck between comfort and security and a readiness to face challenges and take personal risks. The first challenge for many learners is to become actively involved — literally to get out of their seats — at the beginning of the course, being engaged in activity, and then reflecting on that experience. Such activity sets a climate in which people expect to

be challenged. They may feel uncomfortable with that expectation, but be sufficiently reassured by sharing their discomfort with others, and sensing the supportiveness of the group.

6 *Establishes goals and needs* The climate needs to incorporate the starting point of each individual learner. By providing opportunity for people to explore and express their needs, learners begin to feel that they have some control over what is happening to them, and that the course is focused and dependent on them and their experience. Sharing starting points at the beginning creates a climate in which people are prepared to actively review their own progress. It is the first step in making evaluation central to the process of learning, and in involving the learners in evaluating for themselves the learning they have derived from the course.

7 *Shifts the focus* In creating the climate, we are deliberately setting up a situation in which the learners will move increasingly to centre-stage. The focus shifts away from the trainer. This may work against the expectations of many people, who expect the trainer to be the focus of their attention for the majority if not all of the course. Turning the group in on itself, so that people are focusing on themselves and each other, has a profound effect on the nature of the learning environment, and the relationship between learner and trainer.

Managing the climate

In our view, one of the principal tasks of the trainer is to create and maintain a climate that is conducive to learning. We have broken this task down into four stages, each following on from the other:

1 Recognising the existing climate
2 Releasing energy and supportiveness
3 Gaining commitment
4 Consolidating commitment and support

At each stage, the trainer has to take conscious steps to monitor and modify the climate to ensure that the group is ready to progress to different phases, to take part in new activity, and to meet new demands.

Recognising the existing climate

The existing climate is best recognised by observing the way group members behave towards each other. For example:

- If, as the group is settling down, there is loud laughter and shouted greetings, this generally means one of two things. It may mean that people are feeling relaxed and confident in relation to the course and each other. Or it can mean that people are reacting nervously by forming a defensive grouping, in which case there is the potential for resistance or challenge later on. Moving around the group talking to people helps us to check out our assumptions, and to form a clearer picture of the climate that we have to work with. We can then decide, for example, to what degree we will have to establish our authority during our introduction.

- People seem to find hidden messages in how the seating has been arranged beforehand. If they move the furniture, or find a table to sit by, or move their chair further away from the front of the group, they are signalling a need for protection and security. Where and how people sit at the beginning of a course is an indicator of the level of anxiety they are feeling.

- Some individuals don't feel comfortable being part of a group of strangers, or feel excluded if there are small groups of people who know each other. They may sit apart from everyone else, by a window or near the door. Or they may hide behind a newspaper, or busy themselves with some work that they have brought with them. Drawing these people into the group can be difficult. Making brief contact with them beforehand, demonstrating that we are aware of their discomfort, shows them that we are sensitive to their needs and will be supportive of them in relation to the group.

- Some people need to express their lack of commitment to the course early on. Either they don't turn up until the second day, or they come up to you at the beginning to tell you they can only stay for part of the course, or have to leave early, or come late, or that they are expecting an important phone call, and may be called out at any time! However justified, these always seem to us to be aggressive displays of separateness, which can either be contagious, or very irritating for the rest of the group. Either way, we have to find ways of generating some motivation and commitment in such people, before they sour the early climate of the course.

These are only some of the more obvious signals that may be being transmitted before a course starts. Each instance has to be treated on its merits. It is easy to make false assumptions. Going up to people and checking out what they are feeling does not only help to clarify the situation. If they are feeling negative in some way, it can be the first step in reassuring them, or disarming their hostility. Even if there is not time to approach people individually, these early messages need to be taken into account when we first address the group. For example, we may need to shorten our introduction in order to involve people more quickly in an activity which will release energy and tension. Or we may need to say more at the beginning in order to reassure people about the nature of the course, and to demonstrate our capacity to take their needs into account.

Releasing energy and supportiveness

Convention seems to require a formal introduction at the beginning of a course. How the introduction is made has considerable impact on the climate. A certain amount of scene-setting can help to give the course status and credibility. It also provides a settling-down period for the group — a chance to acclimatise to their surroundings. If the introduction goes on too long, however, it can sap the existing energy in the room, dim expectations, and make the move from passive to active learning difficult.

The introduction is the first time that the group will see the trainer at work, a time when they form impressions about the trainer's power and authority which crucially affect their initial attitudes to the course. The way the trainer behaves in these opening minutes tells the group not only what to expect of the trainer, but what the trainer is going to expect of them. We try to 'model' the way we want the group to behave. If we want them to be energetic, we will be energetic and enthusiastic in our introduction. If we want the group to be supportive, we will convey a caring and reassuring attitude. If we want the group to be open, we will be open about ourselves, talking about our own feelings at that time, or making references to our personal lives.

In general, we keep our opening talk as brief as possible. People can become enthused by an introduction, but it can't *release* their energy. For this to happen, they need to be given something to do, something that requires their active commitment. We move on from the formal introduction to an informal stage. The precise nature of this will depend on the group, how well they know each other, for example. But the stage will always consist of physical movement, involving making some form of contact with other members of the group. It may be to rearrange the furniture into a more relaxed and flexible format. It may be to introduce yourself to someone you don't know, or to find out the names of everyone else in the room.

This direct attempt to shift people from a passive to an active mode sometimes comes as a rude shock to people who have been expecting a more conventional learning experience. There are times when no-one wants to move, when people look apprehensive, embarrassed, even hostile. The trainer needs to 'model' what they want of the group, leading the movement, showing the level of energy required, making real contact with people to show that it isn't just a game.

If the existing climate of the group is far removed from the kind of climate we want to establish, reaction at this point will be strong. People may just sit in their seats and refuse to move, or question the purpose of the exercise, or huddle into groups with people they already know. We then have to challenge the existing climate more directly, rather than relying on the activity to move it gradually. We may be able to continue the exercise by asking people to suspend their doubts for later, or by encouraging individuals to become involved. We may have to stop the activity and review the group's responses to it, explaining its purpose, and discussing why people reacted in the way that they did.

The outcome of this stage of the course, whether people are resistant to it or not, is to shift people's expectations, often radically. They realise that they will be actively and energetically involved in the course. They also realise that they will be working closely with other people, and that this interaction will be an area of learning in itself. People have taken steps towards each other, found out about each other, and helped each other. It is at this stage that the beginnings of group supportiveness are established.

Gaining commitment

The process of releasing energy is the first step in moving people from active to passive involvement. The next step is to encourage them to explore their feelings about the course itself, as a way of clarifying expectations and identifying goals. After the flurry of movement following the introduction, people are asked to find a partner to work with through a process of paired discussion. Partners should not know each other well, preferably not at all.

We provide the pairs with an agenda for their discussion, and some indication, as each stage is introduced, of the level of disclosure that we are looking for. But pairs choose for themselves how they respond to the agenda, saying as much as they feel comfortable with. The agenda itself will depend on the situation, but generally moves through immediate issues, such as 'How did you get here this morning?' or 'Have you had to clear your desk of work in order to be here today?', through to talking about professional background and experience, through to more personal biographical issues. Finally, pairs are asked to focus on their hopes, fears and expectations about the course.

The next stage in the process is to move people into bigger groups, usually groups of four. People introduce their partner to the group, having beforehand discussed which parts of the preceding conversation they wish to be disclosed. In this way, participants quickly get to know a small number of people at a slightly deeper level than they would if it was just left to chance.

This attracts commitment on two levels. It gives people an opportunity to examine their expectations and motivation regarding the course. It also gives them an opportunity to work closely with a few of the other participants. Because the essence of that work is support and trust, a commitment is generated, first to your partner and then to your small group. This provides a foundation for a more all-embracing commitment to the course, to the other participants, and to the interactive processes which are the bulk of the course's activity.

Consolidating commitment and support

In their small groups, participants now re-focus on their expectations of the course, in preparation for a full-group discussion. Generally a range of different expectations are expressed. These are recorded and set alongside the goals for the course that we have identified after consultation with the clients. The two lists are integrated, hopefully without too much difficulty. If some participants have expectations which are not incorporated within our goals, we will try to accommodate them within the programme. Sometimes there are expectations that we can't accommodate, either because of time, or because they are too far outside our brief. We will make this clear, explaining our reasons, and if possible suggesting other ways in which people could get those particular needs met.

Having agreed on a set of goals for the course, participants are asked to discuss the ways in which they need to behave towards each other as a group in order for those goals to be achieved. Specifically they are asked to identify a number of ground-rules which they think should govern the group's behaviour — ground-rules such as 'no smoking' or 'confidentiality' are given as examples. The ground-rules of each small group are edited into one list which is discussed by the full group until agreement is reached. The list then becomes a 'contract' for the course.

The process of agreeing goals and a contract, via small group activity, consolidates the commitment that has been generated in the earlier processes. Participants have been offered a degree of control over what is to happen to them on the course. They have articulated and expressed their own needs, and had those needs taken into account. They have helped to establish the climate of the course directly through their contribution to the contract. They have come to feel a sense of ownership in relation to the course, and a sense of shared power in relation to the trainers. Because they are partly responsible for the shape and nature of the course, they have greater investment in it being successful.

The process has usually already formed a bond amongst the small groups. Working on the contract generally highlights people's desire for a supportive climate. At this point it becomes possible to discuss with the group in more detail the notion of giving and receiving support, and its importance as an ingredient of the learning process.

The climate in context

The four stages in creating and managing climate outlined above are stages that we invariably use at the beginning of our courses. We also build in points at which people can reflect on the processes, and on their responses to them. Much can be learned from such reflection about the nature of learning and the need for climate. People become aware of how they have been affected by their involvement in shaping the course, both in relation to the course itself, and in relation to the other participants.

Sometimes, however, the context of a course means that such processes are inappropriate. In most cases this revolves around the time available. We have to weigh the benefits to be gained from spending time on creating a conducive climate against the disadvantage of leaving less time to achieve the goals of the course. If the course only lasts for a day, spending half a day on agreeing goals and ground-rules may not be justifiable. We will use these stages, possibly in a reduced form, on courses that last anything longer than a day.

The problem is different with courses that take place in blocks over a long period. In such cases, the climate needs to be re-established at the beginning of each block. Often on these courses the composition of the learning group is not fixed, and changes from block to block. Participants arriving for the first time at block 2 are walking into an existing climate to which they have not contributed. We enlist the help of the 'existing' group, and involve them in an activity to plan how best we, as a group, can include the newcomers. In this way we try to ensure that the group retains shared responsibility for the maintenance of the climate.

Our approach is not infallible. Its success depends on the nature of the existing climate. If people are resistant and hostile to the course, they may be antagonised by interactive processes which demand energy and involvement. They may refuse to take part. Or they may express their hostility through their declared expectations of the course. Sometimes the processes themselves are sufficient to 'turn people round', to channel their negative energy in a more positive direction, either through the catharsis of having expressed their negativity, or through the mitigating influence of other participants. At other times we have to interrupt our processes to respond to the needs of the group, or of particular individuals.

The processes are in one sense an invitation for people to express their negativity. Some trainers that we have trained regard this as an unnecessary risk. We feel that it is more risky for the negativity to remain unexpressed, and therefore unresolved. It will almost inevitably emerge at some point, often in destructive attempts to sabotage the course. Although it can be uncomfortable to deal with people's negativity head on, especially at the beginning of a course, it is a logical consequence of using the existing climate as the starting point of the process of building a climate that is conducive to learning.

3 Support

The nature of support

One of our objectives in the process of creating a climate is to engender support among the learning group. Support is both a feature of the climate and an element in itself. It is born out of the climate, and then grows to be a dominant feature of the course, a key characteristic in the way that we want people to work and learn together. The processes we use at the beginning of the course are designed to develop an awareness and sensitivity to the needs of others. This is the initial stage in developing supportiveness amongst the group. Our aim is to create a learning environment where participants support each other by sharing responses, encouraging involvement, and enabling action.

Support is multi-faceted. It involves awareness of the need for support, both in oneself and in others. It involves skill and sensitivity in formulating and delivering appropriate support. And it involves courage and openness in asking for and receiving support. It requires a capacity for focusing on others and temporarily relegating one's own needs. It requires an ability to 'hear' the feelings that lie behind what people are saying or doing. It requires the discipline of asking questions, of resisting giving the answers. It requires strength to stay separate, to not become entangled in the feelings of others, to accept those feelings as part of their world view.

Support is not always comfortable. It can be both protective and challenging. It can involve levels of openness and honesty which are unfamiliar to many people. Particularly in work settings, acknowledging a need for support is often seen as a sign of weakness and inadequacy. People generally seem to be unused to asking for or receiving support and tend not to see it as a potential resource for their professional development. When there is a supportive culture within an organisation, this is frequently directed at protecting group identity and cohesiveness rather than challenging individuals within the group in order to support their development. Only occasionally do we work with groups which have a culture which is genuinely supportive of its individual members, which offers them reassurance, encouragement, openness and challenge. Such support doesn't promote dependency and self-sacrifice. It is a liberating catalyst for growth and development. It is this kind of supportiveness that we try to generate among the groups of learners on our courses.

Support and learning

One of the most frequent comments made by people who have been on our courses concerns the sense of self-worth they gained from learning with a group of people who provided support and encouragement. People identify this as a significant contribution that training has made to their personal growth and professional development. The frequency of this reaction to training suggests to us that support is a critical element of learning and development. It is one of the reasons, when we planned this section of the book, that we gave support status as a separate element rather than subsume it under climate, as we had originally intended.

This comment from participants is not an initial response; it is usually made some time after the end of the training experience. It seems that the quality of the relationships between people on a course is often not immediately recognised as an element of learning. We have noticed also that people rarely acknowledge that they have given support as well as received it. But on reflection, people have recognised that support assumes such significance in their recollection of the course precisely because it was reciprocal, because there was the opportunity to receive and give support on an equal basis. It is the reciprocal nature of support amongst peers that, when it is nurtured, gives it its power and significance.

When we ask people to focus on why support was such a critical factor for them regarding the effectiveness of their training experience, they usually respond with one or more of the following five reasons:

1 *Feelings of affiliation* Participants are organised in small groups which work together regularly throughout a course. The effectiveness of the group depends on the contribution and commit-

ment of its members. As the course progresses, the groups develop a strong sense of their own identity. Active learning requires people to make a personal contribution to the course. One of the group tasks is to receive and respect these contributions. In carrying out this task, the group becomes aware of the difference between supportive and unsupportive behaviour. At certain points in the course, groups are asked to reflect on this difference as a way of learning about group-work and group support. The intensity of this learning bonds the group, and generates a powerful feeling of group affiliation.

2 *Motivation to learn* Learning involves change and change is often resisted. People are reassured by sharing their feelings of doubt and anxiety with others. By sharing these feelings, the group starts to overcome them. As they become aware that the group is responsible for its own learning, people support each other to overcome their resistance. Some take the lead, enabling others to follow. The expectation that everyone will contribute generates a motivating force that becomes irresistible. When this expectation is combined with a growing trust in the receptivity and supportiveness of other group members, the group becomes a powerful forum for learning.

3 *Facing challenge* When learners feel supported, they are prepared to meet new challenges. Challenge occurs when the existing framework of the learner is disturbed. Learning which is by nature active and experiential will create such disturbance. The presence and support of the group encourages the learner to accept the challenge of learning from experience. It lends strength to the decisions the learner will make about facing challenge. Resistance can be expressed, validated and overcome. Determination to face challenge is encouraged. The group learns from the different reactions to challenge of its members, and from the way they worked together to help people to overcome their resistance.

4 *Continuing development* The long-term aim of training is to help people to develop both personally and professionally, and for development to continue beyond the training event. Feedback received from participants suggests that receiving support from other learners is a significant factor in providing motivation to continue to learn. People have returned to work and looked for support to continue their own development, and for ways of supporting their colleagues. The members of the training group may

not meet again, but if they have recognised the importance of support, they try to promote it in other groups to which they belong. Even if just two people come together to provide each other with support, we believe that there is greater potential for their individual development.

5 *Reflection* Reflection is crucial to the process of learning from experience and to preparing the learner for new experiences. Structured reflection is difficult to do alone. There is a gap between how people perceive their behaviour and how others have perceived it. Fact and feelings are often mixed up, and memory becomes distorted. It is difficult to articulate emotional responses, and to draw out what has been learned from an experience. Substantial benefits can be gained from group reflection, guided and structured by inputs from the trainer. The group supports the reflection of the individual by providing an objective, non-judgemental ear, by asking questions to release thought, by probing to move beyond thought to a feeling level. Each individual learns from the reflection of others as well as from their own.

Support and the trainer

Traditionally the trainer is regarded as the primary, if not the sole, source of support for the learning group. In active learning, the role of the trainer becomes secondary: to enable the learning group to support each other. Support is given to individuals if necessary, but the main responsibility is to support the groups in their endeavours to become supportive. This is one of the key areas in the shifting of the locus of power away from the trainer towards the learner.

This is often a difficult transition. For many trainers their identity is tied up with being helpful and caring. To move away from that identity can cause them initial confusion and dissatisfaction. But in reality it is difficult for the trainer to provide equal support to each member of their group of learners. Some will demand more of their attention than others. And the quality of the trainer's support is coloured by the authority inherent in their position as leader of the group: encouragement can be perceived as impatience; approval as endorsement.

In active learning, the trainer's role is to guide groups of learners through a process of reflection. This involves providing structure for this reflection, in the form of an activity or an agenda for discussion. The trainer supports the groups by ensuring that each person is contributing to the reflection process, and that their contribution relates to their own experience. The trainer ensures that each person's contribution is received equally by the group, and that any feedback given to people about their contribution is constructive and non-judgemental. And the trainer ensures that each person has the opportunity to reflect on and articulate what they have learned, and to relate this learning to future action.

In this way, the primary source of support is the learners themselves. The trainer's role is to enable that support to become available, and to try to ensure that it is effective. The nature of the support that a trainer can offer is different from that available from fellow-learners. It may seem to be more effective in the short-term, because it draws on the trainer's depth of experience. But if the trainer monopolises the support role, they are in effect inhibiting the potential mutual supportiveness of the learning group. And they are denying the group the opportunity to learn about support and their capacity to be supportive. We believe that the relationship between the learners is more important than the relationship between the learners and the trainer.

The support structure

The secondary support role of the trainer can be divided into two broad functions: creating and maintaining a supportive climate; and providing a structure in which support can be developed and explored. We have looked at the issues involved in creating a climate in the previous chapter. In this section we will focus on our strategy for structuring support.

As always, the amount of time spent on generating and reflecting on support depends on the amount of time available overall. If the training event is of one day's duration or less, there will be no time for focusing directly on support. Learning may be organised in small groups, and there may be some reflection on the process of learning in this way. But if people come away feeling that they have received support, and recognise it as such, this will be incidental. If they make contacts during the day which provide for support afterwards, it is a bonus.

It is possible, if the course is taking place within an organisation, with one or more staff teams attending, that support can be placed directly on the agenda. Activities can be provided which enable people to reflect on the degree and quality of support they receive at the moment and which they would like to receive in the future. They can be encouraged to identify ways in which they could get the support they need, either from within or without the organisation, and to plan the first steps they need to take in order to try and make that support available.

In general, however, we don't plan to incorporate a structured approach to support unless the course is at least of three days' duration. When that amount of time is available, we will invariably incorporate support structures as part of the course programming. The structure we use, although it will vary according to the context of the course, will be based on a set of central processes.

Usually the full group is too large for support to develop, and so the first step is to divide the learning group into smaller units. These smaller units remain as a constant throughout the course, often labelled openly as 'support groups'. The composition of the groups may be pre-planned in consultation with the client. Or it may be a natural progression from the processes used in creating a climate. Groups can select themselves, but our preference, if there is time, is to involve the full group in establishing criteria for forming the smaller units. This can be a difficult process, but it gives people an insight into the purpose and function of the support group.

The support groups are not the only groupings in which people will work during the course. In order to develop a whole-group cohesion and identity, different groups are formed for different activities, with the aim of ensuring that people have some working contact with all the other participants at some time during the course. But people return constantly to their support groups at different points, usually to reflect together on recent activity or experience.

Forming the groups does not of itself mean that support will happen automatically. The trainer has to be aware of the quality of relationships in each group when making decisions about the progression of the course. Time may need to be given over to developing supportiveness within the group before moving on to an activity which involves a high degree of challenge. A balance has to be kept between the cohesiveness of the whole groups and that of the smaller units. Too much time spent together can lead to the support groups becoming too introspective and self-restricting. Too little time and they may fail to establish a clear sense of identity.

Once the groups are established, we move around the room observing and listening to the way people are working together. We will spend some time with each group, joining in on discussions, giving feedback if required, reinforcing the group's role as a support to individual reflection, and facilitating the resolution of any difficulties that may arise. We are also gathering information about each group's readiness to move on to a new stage of challenge and support. The information we look for is the quality of listening within the groups, and the developing awareness of the needs of others. We look for signs of relaxation, of the reduction of anxiety and frustration. We wait for the expression of positive feelings about the group, and for the feelings of accomplishment that come with this positivity. When this happens, we can anticipate a willingness within the group to face new challenge and to plan for future support and reflection.

Support groups and individual learning

The validity of co-operative learning is often questioned by participants on our courses. People are unused to learning in this way. They have established their own learning patterns based on past experience, and do not see how working in groups will be of benefit to them. They fear that learning in groups will inhibit the learning of the individual, that they will get dragged down to the group's lowest common denominator, irrespective of their own capacity to learn and develop. Underlying this is often a feeling that learning which is shared cannot be fully owned by the individual.

This reluctance to break with existing patterns, with an adherence to individualised and competitive learning, is often expressed as resistance, or hostility to the support group itself. For many people, the adjustment to a collective learning pattern will be the greatest challenge that they will experience on the course. Personality clashes and intra-group conflict are a common feature of the early development of a support group. The resolution of such conflict can only be achieved if the group supports its members through their period of adjustment. If the group is successful in managing its early development, the feelings of accomplishment that are generated outweigh people's initial reservations. They learn through experience the benefits that can be gained through group support.

This is not to say that their reservations are invalid. We are not suggesting that group learning is the only effective form of learning. Nor are we saying that individualised learning is ineffective. The two approaches are not mutually exclusive. So much of most people's working lives is spent in the company of other people that the ability to work and learn in a variety of ways, alone or with others, is a key aspect of professional development. We emphasise group learning in our training courses because training provides people with a rare opportunity to learn collectively. It also provides people with an opportunity to review how they currently manage their own development, and encourages them to identify ways in which they can gain support for this development when they return to work. This is one of the ways in which we try to transcend the limitations of training's potential to contribute to professional development: by enabling people to establish an ongoing and realistic support system for their on-the-job development.

4 Stepping

Stepping as a management tool

When a person wants to acquire a new skill or piece of knowledge, or reach an understanding of new concepts and ideas, they tend naturally to approach this learning project in a series of stages or steps which conform to a hierarchy of complexity. Their learning is incremental, one step leading to another. Each step provides the degree of competency necessary to progress to the next one. Anyone who is responsible for helping people to learn also tends to plan and structure the learning so that it is progressive, building in areas of achievement at each step in the progression.

In training terms, stepping refers to the structuring of a training event in such a way as to ensure that the participants experience learning as a series of developments. Stepping affects two dimensions of a course: it affects the shape, giving a sense of movement from a starting point to a conclusion. And it affects the depth, giving a sense of movement from the superficial to the profound. Stepping is like the horizontal and vertical holds on a television set. It is a tool with which the trainer manages the developmental momentum of a course.

Most trainers will, consciously or unconsciously, use stepping as a tool in two ways: first, in planning the overall structure of a training events; second, in organising the activities used during the training event. In both cases, the purpose is the same: to develop confidence in the learner so that they can progress to the next step, or stage of the course. Confidence is developed through achievement, whether that be the accomplishment of a task, or the proven understanding of a concept or area of knowledge. Achievement produces feelings of accomplishment which generate the motivation to progress further. This motivation, combined with confidence, enables the learner to be open and receptive to new demands and challenges. By using stepping, the trainer manages the development of learning by building confidence and sustaining motivation in the learner.

Conversely, a common cause of problems in training can be attributed to poor use of stepping. If the learning group is presented with activities which they find too difficult, their likely response is to feel inadequate or threatened. This may be expressed in the form of resistance, or hostility to the trainer. It may be expressed in a sullen withdrawal of commitment. Confidence will drop, and people will become less open and receptive to facing further challenge. Similarly, if insufficient attention has been given to incorporating opportunities for achievement at each step, the learning group may be denied the feelings of accomplishment which generate and sustain motivation. They will be less able to recognise their own progress, and be less in touch with any development in their confidence.

It can be a struggle for the trainer to take responsibility for these problems, as they often appear to be intransigence on the part of individual learners or the group as a whole. We have recently experienced a situation where we asked people to participate in an activity which was too complex for the stage that had been reached in the course, and for the stage that had been reached in our relationship with the group. The activity was rejected. It was tempting to blame the group, who hadn't been particularly easy to work with anyway. But we both had to accept that it was our fault. We hadn't built in sufficient steps to develop the readiness to embark on such a complex and demanding activity.

The activity was an attempt to get the group to deal with a set of policy issues concerning play provision in a way that involved them on a personal level with some of the people who would be affected by those issues. There was a reluctance within the group to include the personal with the political and we felt that this attitude needed to shift if there was to be a commitment to the outcomes of the course. We should have provided a series of simple steps which acclimatised people to the purpose of the activity, and familiarised them with the kind of skills they would need to carry it out. In fact, building in such steps wasn't possible given the time constraints of the course. We wanted to do the activity because we knew it would be an effective process for achieving some of the multiplicity of goals that had been identified. Our mistake was to be over-ambitious. We forgot to be flexible and stuck to our plan without taking into account the needs of the group.

Planning and flexibility

So far we have talked about stepping as a tool for planning courses and organising activities. In this sense, it is one of the ways that the trainer is proactive. The example we have just given demonstrates that it also needs to be used reactively, in response to the state of the learning group. Unless the group is well-known to the trainer beforehand, it is impossible to anticipate accurately the level of confidence that they will bring to the course. Even with a group that is well-known, it is dangerous to make assumptions about their readiness to face challenge. In our experience, groups usually need to go through steps even if all that the steps do is reinforce areas of existing skill or knowledge. Missing out on opportunities to provide feelings of accomplishment, however much they seem to be going over old ground, can still have a negative impact on the confidence and motivation of the group.

We find that we are constantly adjusting the steps we have pre-planned in order to match the pace of a course to the needs of the learners. Sometimes we have to slow things down by adding steps into a process in order to reassure the group. We need to set a pace with which they feel comfortable. If we are successful, we can accelerate that pace slowly as the course progresses. At other times, we have to remove steps that we thought might be necessary. We had under-estimated the motivation and enthusiasm of the group, who found our careful build-ups frustrating and patronising.

As we gained more experience as trainers, we found that we pre-planned in less and less detail. We had experienced the problems that can come about from a rigid adherence to a plan. And we found that the more time we spent planning, the greater investment we had in our plans, and so the more reluctant we were to jettison them if necessary. We still plan courses, but now may only map out the broad steps that we want to take. We usually plan the first steps of a course in some detail, in order to create the climate we feel is necessary, and to establish our authority with the group. We may identify a range of options for what will happen next, but will only select from those options when we have a clearer sense of the needs and nature of the learning group. In most cases our response to the reality of the course, in practical terms, will revolve around decisions to do with the degree of stepping that we feel is necessary.

The reduced dependency on pre-planning requires an increased flexibility *in situ*. Flexibility develops partly through an expanded repertoire of activities and processes, and a familiarity with that repertoire which allows for adjustment through introducing or withdrawing steps. It also develops through an increased ability to read and interpret the signals being transmitted by the learning group. This ability comes through experience, but requires, in our opinion, a readiness to trust to intuitive understandings of what is happening within the group. Flexibility requires the confidence to let go of the planned structure and, sometimes, to step into the unknown. It requires confidence in your ability to improvise, and to get yourself, and the group, back from whichever unknown you have taken them to.

As we become more flexible, we become more focused on the needs of the learners, less focused on our own needs as trainers. As the focus of attention shifts, we become increasingly aware of any dissonance between the real and anticipated needs of the learners, and increasingly capable of adjusting the planned in accordance with the real. Shift in focus can also lead, as it does in active learning methodology, to a sharing of the responsibility for such adjustment with the learner. This in fact becomes one aspect of stepping: building in the steps by which the learners can take an increasing degree of responsibility for planning the stages of their own development.

Stepping as an element

Each of our five elements overlaps and interacts closely with the others, sometimes to the point where they become indistinguishable. This is especially true of stepping, which is so universal in nature that it in fact underpins the practical application of climate, support, challenge and reflection. Stepping is a tool which the trainer uses to control the emergence of the other four elements during a course. As such it is an integral part of those elements. Stepping is crucial to the development of climate and support within the learning environment. Stepping is crucial in the preparation of the learner to face challenge, and in the providing of structure for reflection.

Describing the broad steps that are the building blocks of our preplanning becomes another way of describing the interconnection of the other four elements. These elements are present all the time, to differing degrees. The steps provide us with guidelines for when to bring one particular element to the fore, when to move from emphasis of one to emphasis of another, and how to keep a balance between the four elements for the duration of the course. They provide a sense of progression which, in general, can be summarised in the following sequence:

1 *Warming up*: the process of creating the climate at the beginning of a course, with particular emphasis on establishing the expectation that people will be actively participating in and contributing to the learning process;

2 *Group-forming*: the transition of emphasis from climate to support, which creates the expectation of challenge and the reassurance of group sharing and support;

3 *Group-working*: as the nature of the learning process becomes established, it is applied to the content of the learning objectives — people work in groups on tasks relating to the content, whilst at the same time further developing the elements of support and challenge;

4 *Application*: challenge now comes to the fore, as the group apply their learning in situations which challenge their preconceptions about themselves, about working with others, and about the nature of the content itself;

5 *Reflection*: this element, although present during the other steps, now becomes the primary focus for the group, enabling them to review their experience on the course and its relation to their real-life experience — it involves individual feedback within support groups, thus challenging further the group's capacity to be supportive;

6 *Winding-down*: this extends reflection into some form of forward- or action-planning: identifying ways of applying new skills or awareness, gaining support, relaying learning to colleagues, considering how to sustain development.

From professional to personal

The above sequence describes the typical shape of an active learning process. It also describes the way in which the dimensions of professional and personal development become complementary. The content of professional development which is being explored during the course is set within a context which is essentially personal and inter-personal. Stepping is used to construct the context, the learning environment, by building a conducive and supportive climate. The processes used to involve the learners in the construction of their learning environment become part of the content. This is acceptable to the group because the steps have gradually revealed the relevance and potential of the learning to be derived from the processes. And so the processes (the personal dimension) can be maintained as the method for exploring the content (the professional dimension).

Stepping is used to gain the commitment of the learners to the idea that content and process are of equal importance to their development. Once commitment has been gained, stepping is used to deepen their experience and understanding of the relationship between the two. The process by which they focus on the content of the course engages them in reflection on the ways in which they learn, in which they relate to other people, in which they seek and give support, in which they face and respond to challenge. Without careful stepping, the complexity of this combination of content and process would appear confusing and intimidating. It would come across, for most people, as too great a challenge of their expectations about the nature of training and professional development.

In short, stepping enables people to understand and accept that personal development is an implicit part of professional development. It enables people to adjust to the demands of active learning approaches so that they can participate openly and energetically, contributing to and taking responsibility for their own and other people's development.

Stepping in practice

Each of the six broad steps that we identified above can be portrayed in detail as a series of smaller steps. The previous two chapters in this section have described our approach to creating a climate and engendering support as a series of incremental steps which build on and develop the existing climate within the group to the point where it is healthy enough for the group to move on. We won't repeat those steps now, but will apply the same method for showing in more detail how the other four broad steps work in practice.

Group-working

This step usually takes up a major proportion of the time available on a course. Learners work in groups on tasks or activities which involve them in making decisions, solving problems, or facing challenges. Part of their work together may be to decide on the tasks for themselves, selecting tasks that are consistent with the learning objectives they have identified earlier, or which they feel will be sufficiently challenging.

The tasks and activities are content-oriented. They are mechanisms by which participants can collaborate, learning collectively about issues affecting their professional lives. The element of challenge may come through the nature of the content — recent examples in our work have involved teamwork skills and teacher appraisal. But more typically, the challenge comes through the process of working together, of sharing responsibility for the completion of the task, and of sharing responses to the task as part of the learning process. Challenge is most frequently explicit after the activity has been completed, when individuals receive feedback from other members of their group.

This step is dependent on there being sufficient support available within the group. From that base, small steps are taken to develop the groups' confidence in their ability to work together: for example, they will be engaged in making relatively straightforward and low-risk decisions before they become involved in making complex, multi-faceted ones. And steps are taken to develop the groups' ability to be reflective: this may involve practice in giving feedback at a simple and impersonal level, or it may involve activities to develop structures for managing group reflection.

The trainer has to balance two elements during this step of the course. They have to ensure that the activities and processes are sufficiently challenging to provide opportunity for learning at a variety of levels. And they have to ensure that the supportive climate is not only sustained in the face of this challenge, but that it develops in practical ways, so that people become actively and skilfully supportive in order to help each other deal with the personal implications of challenge. This is a difficult balance to maintain, particularly as people will be at varying stages on the resistant–receptive continuum. Stepping is highly influential here in building enough confidence and motivation not just within individual learners, but within the several groups, so that they feel comfortable about working and taking risks together.

Application

Application is a continuation of group-working. It is a way of capital-ising on and consolidating the learning which is beginning to emerge as a result of people working collectively. The step involves learners in applying what they have learned on the course to other contexts. It is an opportunity for them to be creative with both the content and the processes that they have been experiencing. The step usually comes at the mid-point in a course, when people are beginning to think about what the course means for them in real terms, what practical value it has for them in their working lives.

Our preference is to provide the learners with real situations with which to apply their learning. Recent examples are the running of a seminar explaining active learning to fellow teachers, and a similar meeting with a group of school governors. The introduction of reality into the slightly unreal world of a training course can come as a rude shock, like leaving a warm bath to jump into an open-air swimming pool. The application is different from normal experience because people are working in groups to both plan and carry out their particular task. They are aware, too, that they will be returning to the safety of the course to reflect on their performance afterwards. But this step in the course represents the greatest degree of challenge to the learners. The challenges they have experienced during the group-working phase have been steps to prepare them, in their groups, for the risk of exposing themselves, first to the outside world, but also, and often more significantly, to the other members of their group.

Application involves learning on a multiplicity of levels, and represents the greatest synthesis of content and process during the course. People engage with the content of the course actively and practically, as much as possible in real settings. They have to become creative with the content in order to integrate it with their previous way of working. They do this with a group of other people, which both provides motivation and denies the possibility of escape; which both provides support and demands support; which both shares the responsibility and increases it. The preceding steps have been steps towards this point.

Reflection

Opportunities for reflection need to be built in to all stages of a course. Every activity includes a period for reflection, however brief. Reflection is one of the ways in which people become aware of the processes being used, and of the incremental nature of those processes. As such, it is an integral part of the stepping process.

On one level, reflection involves the learner in a personal examination of their responses and reactions to their experiences on the course. On another it involves them in giving and receiving feedback. This means that they need to be aware of other people, and of their reactions to other people. And they need to find ways of expressing those reactions in ways which will be experienced as positive and supportive. Similarly, they become aware of their effect on other people. And they need to find ways of receiving feedback from others so that it remains useful to them.

The emphasis on reflection increases gradually throughout the course. This is inevitable as learners have more experience, and more complex experiences on which to reflect. Near the end of the course, however, it comes to the fore in a period given over to reflection on the course as a whole learning experience. This period is given a structure which is divided into five steps:

- *recalling* the details of the experience to date;
- *reflecting* on responses felt at the time, and about feelings felt about experiences at this stage in the course;
- *recording* details of what has been learned for future reference;
- *reviewing* the stage reached in terms of professional development;
- *assessing* future needs.

These steps provide a structure for self-evaluation which can be used to reflect on significant experiences in the future. During the course, they help people to 'come down' after the high of application. They ensure that people don't just reflect on that experience because it is the most recent and most significant. Reflection helps people to see that application wasn't an isolated experience, disconnected from other experiences during the course, but was an extension of those experiences. This period of reflection is one of the ways in which people learn about the function and value of stepping.

Winding-down

Winding-down starts during reflection. In this sense, people have been winding down throughout the course as a way of coming out of one period of intense activity and preparing for the next. During this last step, however, winding-down has an additional function which brings it to prominence. It is planned as a kind of decompression chamber, a period in which learners can prepare to leave the rarified atmosphere of the course and to make their re-entry into the real world.

People build on the last step during reflection by planning how they are going to use what they have learned on the course when they are back at work. The trainer supports the learner to:

- consider the practical application of what they have learnt;
- recognise the importance of support as an element in their learning and development;
- explore the potential for giving and getting support in their work;
- clarify the extent to which their expectations and goals for the course have been met.

Such winding-down activity gives people the opportunity to get the course into perspective: to see it as a short-term and limited intervention in their professional lives and development. This sense of perspective is essential to minimise the risk of people becoming hurt and demoralised when they return to work and the weight of the normative controls of their work experience bears down on the confidence and enthusiasm that has been generated during the course. Not only have people lost the support of the group and of the trainers, but they are back in contact with people who in most cases will not have shared that experience, who will feel excluded from it, and who may well need to reassure themselves by undermining its validity. One of the activities we sometimes use during winding-down is one in which participants roleplay telling colleagues about the course when they return to work. The learners must be made aware of the need to protect themselves, and the steps they have taken during the course, from a world that is usually unsupportive of, if not openly hostile to, such development.

5 Challenge

The concept of challenge

In its broadest sense, learning is a challenge. It challenges the existing state of awareness and understanding of the learner. It challenges the learner to build on the existing, but more especially, to move away from it towards the new, the unknown, to move from security to insecurity. Learning disturbs the world view of the learner. It disturbs their familiar way of seeing, thinking and behaving. It suggests that their way is not the only way, that there are other ways, and it asks that those other ways be taken into account, explored, respected, and if appropriate, incorporated. Learning challenges the learner to change.

People experience challenge and respond to it in different ways. What is seen as challenging by one person may be routine to another. For some people the degree of challenge contained in a learning experience may be daunting, for others it may be only mildly stimulating. No activity or experience is in itself inherently challenging. It is only challenging if it is felt as a challenge. The degree of challenge can be measured by the degree of discomfort that it generates, the degree to which the learner perceives the demand as a risk, a threat to their existing order. It can be measured by the degree of movement it is asking of the learner.

This is true of all learning. But only some teaching strategies actively use challenge as an integral part of the learning process. Such strategies create challenging situations which are central to the learning experience and which form the basis for exploration and reflection. Outdoor pursuits training uses physical challenge in this way. Active learning uses emotional and intellectual challenge to move the learner towards new perceptions of themselves, their colleagues and their work. What both training styles have in common is that they are experiential. Learners learn by doing. Doing holds more risk than listening, reading, understanding and other forms of passive learning. It involves the testing of understanding, the application of understanding and, often the most challenging, it involves exposure to others.

The collective nature of experiential learning is in itself a challenge. Most people are not used to learning which involves interaction with other learners. Nor are they used to taking responsibility for their own learning and sharing that responsibility with others. For some people, the demands of openness and accountability that are made by working in groups will be the greatest challenge they experience on our courses. If the group is made up of people that they work with, the risks are greater. Working with familiar people in a different setting, in different ways, can directly challenge the normative controls of the group, forcing people to expose their assumptions, to see each other in a new light, to move out of the constraints of the expected, to redefine relationships.

Whilst groupwork can be the source of the greatest challenge for many people, it is also the source of the support which can enable them to meet that and the other challenges to be faced on a course. It can be a challenge for some people to seek and receive support, but ironically, and self-evidently, they will need support to meet that challenge. Support provides people with a security which allows them to move into insecurity. The expectation of the group provides them with the motivation to take risks, to face challenges which, alone, they may have avoided. In experiential learning, support is the partner of challenge, as well as being a challenge in itself.

As we have seen in the last chapter, support and challenge are developed incrementally during a course. Stepping is used to build in the learning group a readiness to face challenge based on feelings of accomplishment. The degree of challenge at any one time is attuned to the receptiveness of the group, with the intention of increasing the degree appropriately as the course progresses. In this way, a confidence in the ability to respond to challenge grows alongside an awareness of the benefits to be gained from doing so. From this confidence and awareness comes a motivation to seek out challenge. Our main aim, as trainers, is to bring about a move in the learner from responding to challenges set by someone else to being able and willing to set challenges for themselves.

The importance of challenge

We frequently meet resistance when we confront people with challenges on courses. Why, we are asked, do people need to go through the discomfort of moving into new areas of awareness? Is the risk and disruption really necessary? Why ask people to explore difference when they have been operating quite happily with the existing? Why lead people into insecurity? It is difficult to reassure people about the value of challenge. Often the value only becomes clear once the challenge has been faced. The feelings of accomplishment gained by dealing with a challenging situation need no elaboration or explanation from us.

Hank recently ran a course which involved the group in a highly challenging situation. They were a team of people working together in a complex and pressured environment. Their work was being impaired by interpersonal tension, an accumulation of negativity that was being expressed destructively, behind people's backs and so on. He was working with them to explore ways of preventing the accumulation of negativity. The challenge, some way into the course, was to come clean, to: 'say what you need to say to somebody directly to them, with the group there to support you both'. One person in the group was resistant to this. She couldn't see the point. It was just uncovering things that were best left covered up. It couldn't do anybody any good. Hank asked her to check out how the people who had by then taken the risk of speaking were feeling. They each said how much better they felt, liberated, relieved. She eventually also spoke, with great courage, and experienced the same liberation and relief, the same strong feelings of accomplishment. This is an extreme example of challenge. But the response of the woman is typical. The depth of her initial resistance was an indication of her need to face the challenge, and the benefit she would gain from doing so. There was no way this could have been explained to her beforehand.

But challenge is not just about generating feelings of accomplishment. In our view it is central to the business of development, and one of the key bridges between professional and personal development. In their working lives people reach levels of achievement and effectiveness. Development involves recognising the existing level, identifying the next level, and planning for movement from one to the other. In other words, development, like challenge, is primarily about movement. The movement from one level to another is itself a challenge.

People tend to stop developing when the security they feel in their present level of development outweighs the risks involved in moving to the next. They reach a plateau. Particularly in organisations whose structure and culture do not actively encourage development, such plateaux can be reached early in a person's working life. It is likely that, if people stay on their plateau, their potential to contribute to the organisation will not be realised, nor will they realise the potential that they could gain from their work. They will probably cease to be stimulated by what they do. The recognition they get will become less and less meaningful to them. They will become stale. They will become more callous, less committed to or caring about what they do. The longer they stay on their plateau, the harder it is to take the risk of moving on.

Training, as a structured intervention into a person's professional development, can provide the spur or the catalyst needed to reactivate a person's developmental momentum; or it can provide affirmation and encouragement to those already moving forward; or it can provide a sense of direction or purpose to those who don't know where to go. If the element of challenge is central to the training experience it will provide the learner with the opportunity to face challenge in a structured and supported environment, and the opportunity to reflect on and learn from this experience in a structured and supported way. The course provides an experience of forward movement that the learner can take back with them to the real world. The experience provides them with the motivation and the self-confidence to sustain that movement.

Challenge, on a training course, is a representation of what is possible. The excitement felt on a course by people as they come to grips with a challenging activity or process is not the preserve of the training environment. It can happen in the working environment. The stimulation that people receive by being asked to engage with the unfamiliar, to step into the unknown, can be part of their regular working lives. It is through facing the challenge of new situations, new demands, new responsibilities, new activity, that people develop their repertoire of skills, and the versatility to use that repertoire appropriately. Training can only provide people with a limited amount of challenge, sometimes only challenge of a simulated nature. But it can enable people to learn about challenge. It can develop their ability to face it. It can encourage them to seek it out as an essential part of their professional and personal development.

Responding to challenge

The challenge experienced on a training course is controlled and directed by the trainer, but the step of meeting and accepting the challenge is taken by the learner. In responding to challenge, the learner goes through various stages:

- recognising the challenge;
- choosing whether to respond;
- deciding how to respond;
- making the response;
- reflecting on the experience;
- recognising what has been learned.

Central to the process of learning from challenge is the moment of choice, the evaluation of risk against potential gain. Rejection of the challenge may indicate one of several states in the learner:

- they do not feel able or ready to meet the challenge — it is too threatening, too great a step;
- they want to stay put — they can acknowledge the challenge, but are unwilling to engage with it;
- they do not feel challenged, but are willing to recognise the challenge for other people, and to support them through it;
- they deny that the challenge is there, either for themselves or for others, refuse to respond, and reject the responses of others;
- they have deep core beliefs which are in conflict with what the challenge represents.

Learning is not precluded by any of these ways of stepping back from challenge. The task of the trainer is to encourage and enable the learner to consider the response that they have chosen to make, and to understand its significance. For some people, in certain situations, openly rejecting a challenge may be more challenging than agreeing to meet it. The opportunity to reflect on the response that has been made is as important as the challenge itself. It allows people to review their habitual reaction to challenge, and to consider whether they are over-protective of themselves, or whether they expose themselves to too much risk. It helps people to learn that, in the end, they are responsible for themselves. They choose how to respond. Nobody does it for them.

Challenge in practice

There is an element of challenge in all the learning experiences of a course which is participative, active and experiential. In creating the climate in the opening session of the course, the trainer is inviting the learner to involve themselves actively in the process of learning. For some people, depending on their previous experiences, and on their expectations of the course, this will be perceived as a challenge. They have to choose how to respond: whether to become involved, to actively resist, to withdraw quietly. When they are asked to reflect on their responses to the climate-setting activities, this too can be perceived as a challenge — even as an implied criticism of their response. Again they have to choose how to react: whether to comply with the activity, whether to go through the motions, whether to be open, and how open to be.

As the course progresses, challenges of increasing intensity are introduced. The precise nature of the activity will depend on the objectives for the course and the logistical resources available. They will depend on the nature of the learning group, and on the kind of responses they have made so far on the course. But they all generally involve some or all of the following characteristics:

1 *Performance in front of peers* Certain activities require some form of presentation to an audience, sometimes the rest of the learning group, sometimes people from outside the course. Most people find performing in this way a challenge, especially when the content of the performance is unfamiliar. The challenge lies in exposing yourself to the critical responses of other people, in making yourself vulnerable to them. It may also lie in trusting the other people to be supportive, rather than assuming they will be critical. Or it may lie in allowing yourself to not be perfect, to release yourself from the arrogance of assuming that you always should be.

2 *Giving and receiving feedback* Most activities involve some element of feedback, either in small groups or pairs. The learner is faced with a choice of whether to accept or reject the feedback, whether to ignore it or learn from it. Giving feedback, feedback which is honest and constructive, is often more of a challenge than receiving it. Taking the risk of hurting somebody in order to help them is a challenge that many people prefer to avoid.

Being required to give feedback is a challenge that people seem not to expect to be confronted with on a training course. It is generally seen to be the preserve of the trainer to judge, assess, and give feedback. So not only is it a challenge to their level of openness and supportiveness; it is a challenge to their preconception about the nature of teaching and learning.

3 *Working as a group*   Introducing a task which requires co-operation and teamwork challenges the members of the group in terms of their self-awareness and their ability to interact with others. The task should be sufficiently demanding for the group to have to pool their resources if they are to accomplish it successfully. In trying to achieve an outcome with which everyone feels satisfied, people have to deal with the tension between the interests of the individual and the interests of the whole group. If possible, we construct tasks which involve the group dealing with people from outside the course. The more real the task, the more the group feels committed to and responsible for completing it, and the more likely it is that there will be conflict before agreement is reached. Learners are confronted with the challenge of managing the group dynamics, handling tension and conflict, holding back in the interests of other people, sharing leadership, encouraging others, providing ideas and support.

4 *Applying new learning*   Activities which involve the learner in actively using what they have just learnt challenge them in a number of ways. Application is a rigorous testing of understanding, exposing any laziness or assumption on the part of the learner. It requires them to be creative and imaginative with what they have learnt, rather than passive and accepting. It demands that they take the risk of seeming incapable of assimilating new learning. And it challenges them to make links between the course and their work, to see the potential in what they have learnt for their everyday experience. Application forces people to see the implications of their learning, and thus challenges them to review their pre-course experience in the light of that learning.

5 *Choosing personal challenge*   On some courses, if appropriate and practically feasible, we will ask the learner to identify a task for themselves that they will find personally challenging. The task may be completed during the course, or between two stages of a split course. It must involve the learner in a new level of self-awareness or self-exploration. It may, for example, be a task that

someone has been avoiding doing for a long time. It may be to open up a difficult issue for discussion amongst colleagues. The identification and articulation of their individual task is the first step in a process which builds support through group discussion and planning. The group members also challenge each other to ensure that they are being honest with themselves and the tasks they are choosing. The group will meet again to report back and reflect on the experience. The process of choosing personal challenge on a course is a step towards people choosing to identify and face challenges for themselves outside the training scenario.

Challenge and the trainer

The trainer has to constantly evaluate which level of challenge is appropriate at any one time during a course. They have to be flexible and creative in finding ways of presenting challenging activities so that they are perceived by the learner as being challenging but not threatening. The challenge must not seem to be gratuitous. It must be presented and explained as an integral part of the learning process of the course.

We often find it difficult to position ourselves in relation to the group once we have set them a challenging task or activity. It is a time when we feel anxious — anxious that the group might reject the activity; anxious that the challenge may be inappropriate, even damaging to some people. More than ever, we need to stand back from the group, and let them find their own individual responses to the challenge. To trust that they will, and to respect the responses that they make. We need to show that our support is available, although it is easy to be over-supportive because of our anxiety.

Once the group is engaged they tend to look on us only as resources, asking for clarification or specific pieces of information or advice. We need to make sure that they are clear. But we also need to check out that people are stretching themselves in response to the challenge. We watch groups working to gauge their level of commitment and intensity. If we feel that an individual or small group are going through the motions, we will find a way of challenging them, of asking them to re-examine their responses, to look whether their approach will enable them to derive the maximum learning from the experience.

The trainer's principal role is to ensure that sufficient time is available for groups to reflect, at different points in the process, on what they are learning from it. This is often one of the elements of challenge in the process. It is important to allow the learner to express themselves fully, and to provide a structure for their reflection which allows them to review their experience from a calm and more detached perspective. It is vital, at this stage, that the trainer is in no way prescriptive, telling the learner what they should have learnt, or what the exercise was really about. The learning that comes from challenge is highly individualised. People learn about themselves. What they learn may be hard, uncomfortable, disturbing. But it must not be invalidated. Better to leave people with the discomfort than to dismiss their experience in any way, however well-meant. The trainer must find a balance, supporting people through their reflection without taking their learning away from them. Finding the balance is a challenge for the trainer.

6 Reflection

Reflection and learning

Reflection is an umbrella word that we use to describe the way in which people learn from their experience. It is not the preserve of the training course. People do it all the time. Everyone has their own way of processing experience in order to understand it, to give it meaning, to learn from it, to inform future action and behaviour. At an unconscious level, reflection is an automatic human response to experience. At a conscious level it is less automatic. People tend not to reflect on all experience equally. They tend to reflect more on experiences that they have found to be intellectually or emotionally stimulating. They may even shut off from experiences that have been too emotionally stimulating, or wait until they have reached a calm place before looking back. And often, people don't have the time to process all of their experience. New experiences keep crashing in!

Not only is the degree of reflection normally haphazard. The nature of the reflection also tends to be random, unstructured, and governed by the emotional impact of the experience. People don't usually plan how they are going to reflect on a given experience. They may allocate themselves a specific time to think something over. But they rarely decide on a structure for their reflection which is appropriate to the nature of the experience. People develop reflective patterns which they tend to assume are the only way that they can reflect on their experience. More often than not, these habitual reflective processes serve to protect, rather than to challenge, the individual. Even when people share reflection with friends, for example, they rarely consider how best to use their friend as a resource to aid their process of reflection.

In short, left to their own devices, people tend to learn from their experience in a random and unstructured way. A training event is an opportunity for consistent, structured and supported reflection: partly because the purpose of the event is to provide a concentrated dose of experience to learn from; partly because the trainer can provide an external structure for reflection; and partly because there are other people sharing the same experiences, who can support each other through the reflection process.

Structured reflection has two functions: to enable the learner to interpret the personal significance of an experience and to enable them to integrate the learning into everyday experience. It is during the reflection process that the professional and personal dimensions merge, as the learner engages in an exploration of the personal implications of learning which is ostensibly concerned with their professional life. And it is during the reflection process that the connection between learning and future action is made most explicit, as the learner engages in the identification of the appropriate future application of what they have learnt on the course. If training doesn't provide opportunity for reflection, people will reflect in their normal random and unstructured way, focusing on some experiences and not others, and perhaps interpreting those experiences in order to uphold rather than to challenge existing perspectives. And without structured reflection, the transfer of learning from the course to real life will be minimal and vulnerable to learning decay.

Interpretation

A training course is an isolated event in a person's life. It comes and goes, often a quite unreal experience, disconnected from the reality of everyday existence. We have found that people rarely come to a course with clear expectations, or with a clear sense of how the course fits in with the rest of their life. They tend to see it as time off: a chance to stand back, a chance to learn, a chance for a breather. They don't usually see the course as part of their continuing learning process. When we ask people to take some time at the beginning of a course to consider what their expectations are, we are asking them to reflect on their previous experience: the immediate experiences that affect how they are feeling in the present; and their previous learning experiences that affect their expectations of the course. This is the start of the structured reflection process.

So much happens on a course, especially courses longer than a day, that by day three people find it hard to remember what they were doing on day one! Whenever possible, we make time available for people to reflect on a particular process or activity immediately after it has been completed. Reflection, like all the other elements, is stepped. This is partly inevitable: there is less to reflect on at the beginning of a course than there is at the end. But it is also designed to allow people to become familiar with the process of structured reflection, and to use it more and more profoundly as the course progresses.

The final stage of the course is given over to reflection. The learners usually work in support groups through a process which involves:

1 Helping each other to remember all the events during the course. This may include events that occurred during social time, especially if the course was residential, but generally focuses on the teaching and activities that took place during formal course time. The groups are encouraged to compile an accurate and complete list of events.

2 Recalling and sharing individual responses to events as they happened: recalling, for example, how each person felt on the morning of the first day, when they were asked to articulate their feelings about and expectations of the course, and sharing that remembered feeling with the rest of the group.

3 Up-dating responses by sharing with the group their feelings now about events that took place earlier. For example, someone may have felt resentful at being asked to clarify expectations at the beginning of the course. By the end, they may be in a better position to understand the purpose of that exercise: their feelings about it may have changed. As people become used to the process of reflecting on experience, and more trusting of their support group, they tend to become more open about their responses. Updating allows people to speak in more depth, or more honestly, about their feelings regarding earlier events.

4 Selecting from all of the remembered experiences those that they found most personally significant. The group can play an important part here in checking out people's reasons for their selections, and also in giving feedback about their perceptions of each other's responses. It sometimes helps to give groups a target: the three most significant experiences, for example. This works against blanket responses such as: 'they were all equally significant', and forces people to be more rigorous in their self-appraisal.

5 Articulating the significance of the selected experiences. By expressing why certain experiences were significant, or more significant than others, people consciously explore the learning content of those experiences, and, in particular, what they have learnt about themselves.

6 Recording the outcome of reflection. Recording reflection helps learners to clarify and summarise the content of their discussions. Group reflection can be recorded in a number of ways: a group summary on a flip chart, a taped group discussion, a symbolic chart or drawing, a group presentation, a written interpretation of what another person has said . . . these are some of the possibilities. Asking the learners to devise and record their own questions or agendas after an activity is a useful strategy for involving them actively in thinking about the process of reflection. Asking them, in pairs, to devise a way of helping another pair to reflect on their learning is an even more effective way of focusing attention on the reflective process itself.

Integration

Learning, however significant or profound, is not automatically usable. Training which sets out to blur the edges between personal and professional development needs to ensure that participants connect what they have learnt to their working lives. Ideally this connection should be on both a professional and personal level, so that people see implications for themselves in terms of their work, in terms of their relationships with their colleagues, and in terms of their life outside work.

Through interpretation of experience, people will have begun to make conceptual connections, understanding how what they have learnt on the course can apply to their working lives. But this does not necessarily mean that they are in a position to make that application happen. The process of integration is one of making explicit the perceived connections between learning and work. There are generally five phases in this process:

1 Drawing conclusions about the significance of the course within an individual's developmental continuum. By interpreting the personal significance of the learning that has taken place, the learner can gain an overview about their professional develop-

ment, recognising how far they have developed to date, and perceiving the scope and nature of future development. People may identify skills that they want to develop, areas of their existing work that they want to focus on or move into, even areas of work that they can't do in their present situation. By becoming clearer about the way they manage their development at the moment, they can identify changes that they could make, ways in which they can become more proactive, so that they are more in control of the nature and pace of their development.

2 Turning conclusions into actions. Often the conclusions that people come to are of a general nature: large-scale or non-specific changes that they would like to see happen. The changes won't happen unless the learner takes specific action to make sure that they do. Participants are asked to identify specific steps that they can take on their return to work.

3 Ensuring that the steps identified are steps that can be achieved. People, especially if they are enthusiastic at this stage in the course, tend to be over-ambitious, planning action that will be difficult to carry out, and which is likely to fail. If this happens, they will be denying themselves the feelings of accomplishment necessary if they are to sustain their motivation to change. And they are opening themselves to becoming disillusioned at their failure to have any effect. This disillusion may be directed at the course, undermining what learning has been gained. It may be directed at the workplace, souring the learner's relationship with their work. Or it may be directed at the learner themselves, undermining their confidence in their ability to control or effect their working lives. The concept of stepping is useful here in helping people to identify specific and achievable ways of applying their learning. If people have identified generalised or ambitious actions, they can be asked to plan out the steps they will need to take to ensure that those actions will be successful.

4 Making commitment to take action. Making commitment to take the steps that they have identified often involves the learner in a further stepping process, as they come closer to the realisation that these steps are a real possibility, and that it is their responsibility to decide whether or not to take them. When this realisation sinks in, and they start to visualise themselves doing what they have planned, they will, if necessary, break their plan into even smaller and more realistic steps. Asking people to clarify the first step they will need to take, is a useful way to help them do

this. The role of the support group or partner is important here in checking out the practicability of what people are planning to do.

5 Identifying sources of support. If some or all of the course members work together or for the same organisation, they can plan on the course how best to support each other to take the steps they have planned when they return to work. If they have all come from different organisations, the support groups may be in a position to meet together after the course in order to continue supporting their members. If this is not practical, people need to identify sources of support which can encourage and help them to carry out their action-plan. This may in fact be their first step. It may also be their most important step, especially if they are unused to seeking or receiving support in their work.

This action-planning stage of the course is crucial to the process of transition back to work. It helps the learner to integrate their learning into their immediate future. It also helps them gain a more pragmatic perspective on their working life. The course may have affected their anticipation of returning to everyday existence in a number of ways. It may have led them to feel dissatisfied with themselves and the work that they have been doing up to now. It may have led them to feel disconnected with the organisation that they work for, the lack of support that is available to them, for example. It may have led them to feel despairing about the possibility of ever changing their working life for the better. People are often excited and stimulated by a training experience, not just because of the quality of learning, but because of the opportunity to take a break, stand back, meet other people, compare notes and so on. There is a danger that their positive enthusiasm at the end of a course can plummet into negative disillusionment when they return to the grim reality of everyday existence. By ensuring that the plans for change that each person has made have taken into account the nature of that reality, people regain a more balanced perspective before they return to work. This in turn mitigates against too violent a swing of the pendulum from optimism to despair.

The learning outcomes of reflection

Interpretation and integration are practical and immediate benefits that can be gained from a process of structured reflection during a training course. But reflection is not solely a retrospective method of making sense of and maximising the potential for learning from experience. It is a source of learning in its own right. Through the process of reflection, people learn about:

1 Their capacity for openness. The quality of reflection is dependent on the degree of openness and honesty that people contribute. Working in small groups to reflect on and review shared experiences creates a demand for openness. If support has been adequately developed during the course, it also provides a safe arena for people to take the risk of being open. Some people will be more open than others, more honest about their feelings about themselves and the other members of the group. The contrast in levels of openness is unavoidable within the close proximity of the group, giving people opportunity to review their attitude to open interaction, their capacity to change their level of openness, and the potential benefits to be gained from being more open.

2 Their capacity for learning from experience. When people are actively engaged in reflecting on a course, they become aware of their habitual responses to experience, and the degree to which those responses may have previously promoted or hindered their development. Working with other people, observing the ways in which they engage with reflection, provides the learner with comparisons with which to review their own learning style. Self-perceptions are checked out, and sometimes challenged; responses are queried or affirmed; experiments with new behaviour are encouraged and supported.

3 Their capacity for independent learning. One of the tenets of our approach to training is that people learn most effectively when they take responsibility for their own learning. The full meaning of this only becomes truly apparent to the learner during the process of reflection, and particularly during the integration phase. It becomes clear, as people plan how to use what they have learnt, that whether they do so or not is entirely their responsibility. No-one can make them do anything. After the course they are on their own. They don't have to be: they can

seek out the support of others. But the decision to do so is likewise their responsibility. In planning what action to take, people become aware of their capacity for independent learning. Their resistance, or cynicism, or pragmatism, or over-ambition is revealed by the nature of the steps they have identified. Group involvement in this planning phase provides a source of feedback which heightens self-awareness.

The trainer's role

Initially the trainer's role involves planning the course to ensure that there is sufficient time available for reflection, and making sure that the time made available is used for that purpose. This sounds disarmingly simple, but in our experience, it is always a struggle to safeguard the time set aside for reflection. However much time we allow for activities and exercises, people always seem to need longer! Combining learning activity with reflecting activity is difficult for the group. We are pulling them forwards by asking for their active involvement in an activity, and then asking them to step backwards to reflect on their responses to it. The emotional states required are different. People often have to suspend their reflective selves in order to engage fully in the activity, become energised and enthused during it, and are on an emotional high when they have completed it. Reflection requires them to be calm, thoughtful and sensitive. People need time to move between these two contrasting states: they can't switch immediately from one to the other.

One of the ways of managing this transition is to use a variety of approaches: people reflecting on their own, in pairs, in small groups, or as a whole group; people reflecting by writing, talking, drawing, demonstrating or planning ways of helping other learners to reflect on the preceding activity. Such variety helps to prevent reflection being seen as the 'downer' at the end of intense activity. In many cases, it becomes an intense activity in itself. The structure of the agenda for reflection should allow for exploration of emotional as well as intellectual responses. It may help to step the agenda so that people start by focusing on intellectual responses, which they generally feel more comfortable with, before moving on to sharing their feelings. The need for stepping will change as the group becomes more familiar with, and experienced in, the reflection process.

Having organised and structured the time given over to reflection on a course, the trainer's role becomes less easy to specify, depending largely on the nature of the learning group and their reaction to the requirement for reflection. It is one of the times on a course when the trainer has to operate primarily from their intuition, gauging if, when and how to become involved in the work of individuals, small groups, or the group as a whole. They will need to be sensitive to the climate, judging the appropriate degree of challenge and support to look for. And they will need to be sensitive to the needs of individual learners, judging whether to push people further or support and affirm the steps they have taken. Their contributions or interventions should be in the form of questions which lead people towards further reflection — moving from an intellectual to an emotional consideration, for example. They may need to model the level of openness that they think is appropriate for the stage of the course by sharing some of their own responses.

The trainer does not have to hear each person's responses to the agenda for reflection. It is more important that each person has an opportunity to make a contribution. The trainer's role is to provide the framework for discussion and then to move around, listening in on the work of the various groups, and gaining an impression of the overall content and quality of the contributions being made. In doing this, the trainer can evaluate how far to take the process at each stage, cutting short reflection which isn't fruitful, or changing direction where necessary. In summary, the trainer's role is purely one of facilitator. Intervention should be kept to a minimum, and directed at moving the group into a more profound level of self-exploration.

There are, however, two behaviour traits that we watch out for when people are engaged in reflection and feedback, and which merit intervention. The first is when someone reinterprets what other people have said, thus invalidating the original, or negating someone's experience: 'So what you're really saying is . . .'. The reinterpretation needs to be checked for accuracy — it may say more about what the second person is feeling than about the original. Asking the interpreter whether that is in fact what *they* feel helps shift the focus on to them and validates the statements of the original speaker.

The second is when people generalise their responses, assuming that everybody feels the same. This is frequently indicated by the avoidance of the first person singular, for example 'You know how it is, when you do this kind of thing on a course, you behave totally differently than you would do in real life!'. These are seductive statements and need to be resisted. One way is to ask the rest of the group whether they share that perspective. Another way is to ask people to say 'I' when they are talking about themselves. This is surprisingly difficult for most people to do, and things tend to sound very different: 'When I do this kind of thing on a course, I behave totally differently than I would do in real life!'. Our most frequent intervention during reflection is to get people to personalise their responses instead of generalising them. Asking people to say 'I' is one of the clearest ways of demonstrating to them the basic difficulties in taking responsibility for yourself. It is often a microcosmic representation of what the whole course has been about!

Section Four: Learners Are Only Human

Introduction

In Section Two, we talked about some of the implications for a trainer in using an active learning approach. In the last section, we looked at what we regard to be the key elements of the active learning process. So far we have focused on the trainer's end of the business. We haven't talked much about what goes on for the learner, or if we have, only in terms of how that affects us as trainers.

An active and participative learning approach tends to define the nature of the relationship between trainer and learner. The learning process tends to reinforce that relationship. It is one that is essentially equal, where power and responsibility are shared, and where that sharing is seen as integral. The trainer manages the learning environment. The learner manages their own learning. This is the ideal. We work to achieve that ideal. But it is *our* ideal, our perception of what is the best, the right way to enable people to learn. That perception is not always shared by the learner: shared both in the sense that they may not be aware of the premises that underpin our work; and in the sense that if they are aware of it, they may not agree with it.

Some learners come onto our courses expecting to be 'taught' in the old-fashioned sense of the word. They don't expect to be actively engaged in their own learning. Others come *hoping* that they will be 'taught'. They don't *want* to be actively engaged in their own learning. People develop learning styles which derive from their previous learning experiences, from the kind of person they are, and the kind of life they have lived. Their preferred learning style doesn't always tie in with our preferred approach to training.

The learner is the third dimension of the training scenario. And it is a dimension that is of equal importance to the other two: the trainer, and the learning process. It is easy for us, as trainers, to lose sight of this, to focus on the first two dimensions at the expense of the third. We tend to forget that learners are only human; or to see them only as learners, not holistically, as people with a life outside the course; to forget that the course is only ever going to be a small part of that life.

People bring with them onto a course a whole set of feelings. Some are generated by earlier learning experiences and the expectations that have arisen from them. Some are to do with what they understand to be the purpose of the course. Some are to do with their feelings towards the other participants. Some are to do with how they feel about themselves at the moment, either professionally or personally. Some are to do with what happened that morning, yesterday, or last week.

In the introduction to Section Two, we referred to the 'emotional sub-text of the trainer's job'. In Section Four, we explore the emotional sub-text of the learner. Because this is a book for trainers, the emphasis of the section is on the impact that this sub-text has on the learning process, and on the ways that we, as trainers, accommodate the feelings of the learner.

Section Four focuses on three areas:

1 The needs and motivation of the learner
2 The need to resist learning
3 The need for confrontation

It is a response to some of the questions we asked ourselves after we had started working on the book: how do you motivate people to learn? What is the connection between motivation and need? Why do people resist learning? Why do some people seem to need to confront the trainer? What should you do about it?

Because the book is for trainers and about training, there is a danger that it could become a bit self-obsessed. This section is an attempt to redress the balance: to put the learner back in the frame. It is important to do this because we know that, however worked out we are, however confident we feel, we can't totally plan for the reactions of the learner.

As in Section Two, we have used the questions that we identified above as a structure for reflecting on and interpreting our own experience as trainers. Section Four is an edited transcript of a conversation between the two of us. It is divided into three chapters, each dealing with one of the issues listed above. At the end of each chapter there is a summary which leads into a set of activities. You can use these activities as a way of reflecting on the chapter, and of relating its content to your own situation and experience.

1 Needs and motivation

A trainer can usually sense, right at the beginning of a course, that some people are more motivated to learn than others. It may be that some aren't motivated to learn at all. What factors contribute to the learner's motivation? Are they purely intrinsic, to do with their needs as people? Or are there extrinsic factors? And if so, which of these factors can be influenced by the trainer? And how?

H: Do you feel you need to motivate people in some way before they come on the course? Do you send them pre-course material which you hope will have a motivating effect, for example?

J: I think people should receive information about the course before-hand. But that's more to do with them having clear expectations about what's going to happen to them. And they need to get information direct from us, because if we left it to their senior managers — well, in my experience, you can't rely on the senior managers to communicate clearly about a training course. They take the wrong messages back, and they give people the wrong idea.

H: So you will always communicate directly with every participant before a course to ensure that people are coming with appropriate expectations?

J: Yes. I send them an outline programme which states the over-riding aims of the course and the specific objectives for each part of the course when it happens. This gives them an idea of how they'll be working together. And if they actually read the pro-gramme carefully, they'd see that they will be going out some of the afternoons to teach in each other's schools. But that always comes as a surprise to them, always. So we know that they don't read the programmes that carefully. They skim through them, at best.

H: But it's still worth sending the information out to them?

J: It creates a basis for working with them. At the beginning of the course the objectives they were sent are put up on a flip-chart, and we say: 'You've been sent these objectives, but can we still look at them now to see if our expectations connect with yours?'.

H: And what happens if they don't, if they haven't read the blurb and they're not interested in your objectives?

J: I have a lot of debates with our trainers about negotiating around objectives. They say: 'So where does the negotiation come in? You're telling them what the objectives are'. I've never been able to reconcile that, because until I actually meet those people at the beginning of the course, I've never had any contact with them in order to be able to negotiate with them. Their position is always negotiated for them. It's always the senior management that I have to negotiate with.

H: Most of the time I experience people as not being clear about their objectives for a training experience — their personal objectives. It comes as a surprise to people when I ask them to articulate their expectations of the course. They have to spend quite a lot of time thinking about it before they can articulate it. I sometimes wonder whether it's because they've been sent information about the course beforehand. They don't expect to have to work out their own needs because they've been told clearly what it's all about in the literature. Although I'm with you, I don't think they read it that closely. So maybe they just don't have time to think about it!

J: Do you think that asking them to articulate their expectations is a step in motivating them or increasing their motivation to learn from the course?

H: I think so, on two counts. It helps them to clarify for themselves why they are there, and what they could get out of the situation, so they set themselves targets for the course, or get a sense of how they could benefit from it. And I think it's about ownership for them, as well, in that they feel that they can have a say about the course, that they have some power in the situation, and I'm not just going to force my objectives onto them.

J: So to ask you your question, which I didn't answer, what happens if they don't like your objectives?

H: I have got into binds about how much I'm prepared to negotiate with them. I remember one series of courses I ran — we used to have a session with the group about two weeks before the course proper where we discussed, among other things, the goals for the course. One of the trainers, running one of these induction sessions, renegotiated the programme because a large percentage of the group wanted to deal with an issue which we weren't planning to cover. That caused us quite a few problems because it took us into an area which we weren't supposed to be dealing with at that time. I wouldn't have done that. I wouldn't have said: 'OK, we'll change the programme'.

J: How would you have dealt with that?

H: Negotiation is not about giving in. It may be that we can't meet their needs, and we have to be open about that. It seems to me negotiation is about an opportunity to meet as many needs in the situation as is possible, and for people to feel that they have some power in that process. That's different from them having all the power. I usually say: 'This is what I'm intending to do on this course. Does that tie in with your needs?'. And if people have got other needs, I will try to fit them in. But if I can't, I'll ask them to let go of those needs at the beginning. I'll say: 'I'm sorry, I don't think you will get that out of this course. Can you let go of it now, so it doesn't get in the way of you getting other things out of the course?'. Otherwise people can hang on to unmet needs as a way of sabotaging any potential benefit they could get from the course.

J: I prefer to call it consultation rather than negotiation. It's a way of signalling to people the nature of my relationship with them. I am open to consultation. I am not holding on to all the power here.

H: I do think that the consultation process gives people a sense of ownership, and that giving people a sense of ownership motivates them. It's a motivating factor. But I have difficulty with the word motivation, if it is meant just as a sort of abstract drive that propels people through an experience. Because people's motivation is surely made up of a number of complex needs, some of which are to do with learning, some of which are to do with their reactions to the other people, some of which are to do with their feelings about themselves.

J: Why do you find that difficult?

H: I used to think that if people feel a need to learn something, they will be motivated to learn it. But I'm not so sure any more. I tend to think that although that is true, there is another level of needs that people have, and at that level, their needs can be obstructive. People have more ingrained needs, such as vanity, insecurity, competitiveness, which work against their motivation to learn.

J: Are you saying that people can have a motivation to learn and at the same time close off their options for learning? They may be both motivated and anxious, for example?

H: Their need to protect themselves will conflict with their motivation to learn. And however much they rationally perceive a need for that learning to happen, there is a whole set of emotional needs which can block that learning from happening. I become increasingly aware of people's fears, their anxieties, their need for display, their need to be accepted. Because, however motivated they are, those needs of theirs have the capacity to conflict with their motivation, and undermine their openness, and restrict their ability and capacity to learn.

J: I find that distinction you make interesting. I have strategies for generating motivation, and I can see that what I'm doing is tying into a particular set of needs. For example, I find that a powerful motivating force is to involve the learners in being creative. I work from the very beginning towards that end, to get them to be creative with the processes that we've been showing them and involving them in. Early on in the course I will seek ways in which they can get to grips with the processes themselves, using them to solve a problem, or applying them in specific contexts. And I find that is very influential in increasing motivation. They become absorbed, and excited, and totally involved.

H: So the motivation there is about generating a positive energy: active, creative, productive. Or is it about channelling the energy along positive lines, so that it doesn't have the chance to be expressed negatively?

J: It's providing positive channels, yes. But it's not just to do with setting tasks. The activity is task-oriented, but it is the element of creativity that is important. I have to work very hard, moving around all the time, to get people going on the task. But once they get going, that's it — there's no looking back. It sets up a momentum which can last for the rest of the course.

H: I can see that it can generate enormous energy. But is that the same as motivation, do you think? Are they motivated to learn from those activities? Or are they just glad to have an opportunity to invest their energy in something?

J: It's not just about energy, because they are finding out about the processes, and how they work, and how they can be used. For example, I'll put them in pairs or small groups, and ask each group to come up with a scenario, like: 'Think of the worst question you could possibly be asked about this work that we're doing, and write it down'. And then they swop their question, or whatever, with another group, and I say: 'Now work out how you're going to tackle that'. So yes, it releases a lot of energy, but it's absolutely relevant to their experience, so it's directly useful. The other thing that is happening is that they are having a go, and so they begin to believe that they can use these processes. And that boosts their motivation to learn.

H: So the motivation comes through an active engagement in the creative resolution of true-to-life problems? They are beginning to see for themselves the benefits they can get from the course?

J: That's the key. I think ownership and power are important. But I think it's more important that people directly experience, early on, what it is they're going to get out of being on the course, and how it is going to be useful to them in real life. And they also need to feel early on that they can do it, that it's within their capabilities. Then they will be motivated. And you're right. They are then less likely to need to be negative.

H: Does that depend at all on the nature of the course? For example, if you go into a school to work with the staff of that school, is there a difference to courses where teachers from different schools come together in a residential centre somewhere?

J: There is a big difference, yes. There is a far greater potential for people to change on off-site courses. We've had people who have come away from their place of work and undergone quite radical change. It's as if they have been looking for an opportunity to change, and the course provides that opportunity, because the normative controls that operate in their daily situation aren't there.

H: Do you think that people can't face themselves critically within their normal situation, that that wouldn't happen on a course run within their school?

J: Not in every case, but as a general rule. It's to do with how they are perceived by their colleagues, and the weight of those perceptions. They become trapped in a self-fulfilling prophecy, so that even if they want to be perceived differently, they can't break out of it. People are pigeon-holed. Especially in institutions, and especially people who are in positions of authority, or people who have been there some time, so that the myths have built up.

H: And changing the situation so that they become a learner rather than a manager for a while isn't enough? Is that reflected in the level of motivation? When you go into a school to work with the staff is the motivation there different from off-site courses?

J: Usually in my experience there is more negative motivation or apathy. Usually the majority of people aren't motivated at all. There will be a sprinkling of people who are, but in my experience it is very difficult to get them to come out in the open with it.

H: How do you go about generating motivation in those situations?

J: I start by giving everybody the opportunity to say what they feel about why they're there and what we're trying to do in the day. I'll structure it by asking them to have a conversation with somebody else, and the agenda leads up to them telling their partner about their expectations of the day. Then I'll put them into groups of four to share their conversation with another pair, but I deliberately create groups of people from different departments or teams. Then I'll give the groups an activity, which might be to rank different statements about the day in order of importance, or to complete a set of open-ended phrases. The whole point of this tight structure is to let them get things off their chest. It doesn't always work, but it usually helps. Often, I as the trainer, the outsider, will get challenged at that point, and some real hostility comes out. I've deliberately created an environment to allow that to happen, so it's not surprising. But I find them very anxiety-making and arduous training events to run because I go in knowing that I'm going to draw the flak. And I have to gear myself up to take it and absorb it.

H: But you see the strategy of enabling people to express their resistance, or their doubt, or lack of motivation as the first step in motivating them? Expressing their negativity doesn't just confirm that they were right to be negative?

J: Well, it might do for some people, I suppose, but when you're dealing with a group of about sixty people, you win some and you lose some! The process is necessary because issues come out of it that really do need dealing with. It may be that they can be dealt with later on. Or it may be that you have to deal with them there and then if you are going to get anywhere. I think if you don't deal with the issues, *that's* when people's negativity is confirmed.

H: Right.

J: The other thing that happens sometimes is that there will be a very strong challenge made, which is really aimed at the senior management, or a member of the senior management. But it comes through me, and if I can channel it, that energy, that hostility, once it's been expressed and absorbed by me, and accepted — because I don't react to it, I don't come back at them — it goes away. It's almost like I swallow it all up. And once somebody's dumped it, unloaded their negativity, it actually diffuses things. Not completely — people will still simmer away throughout the day. But it allows some of the people who are motivated to start playing a part. That's the other step in creating motivation: to identify where there is some already, and let it come out so that you're not dealing with the apathy, or negativity, or hostility on your own.

H: So the process which you've described releases an energy for people which might be negative. But through the process of release, the negative energy will either be expended or channelled into positive energy?

J: Most of the time. But one of the problems with on-site courses, certainly with schools, is that they are usually just one-day courses. So a much lower set of outcomes is expected. Sometimes, once they have identified the issues, we give them the opportunity to meet in their normal work-teams. It might be 'year-teams' meeting with the Head of Year, for example. And at some stage in the day we will structure a session which allows them to look at themselves as a team, and address the issues that concern them. We may get them to identify the demands a Head of Year can reasonably make on a team of tutors. And then get them, as a group, to identify the demands that the team of tutors can reasonably make on the Head of Year. We will get them to face those issues head on, usually towards the end of the day, when they're more relaxed, more prepared to say what they think. But maybe the only outcome we'll get is that people have an opportunity to get things off their chest, and that, as a consequence, senior management will have a more realistic understanding of the feeling of the staff towards the issues involved. That's still a positive outcome.

H: One of the differences in motivation between off-site and on-site training, it seems to me, is that there is an extra stage where you have to counteract the prevailing patterns of group behaviour and set up new patterns. Whereas on off-site courses, you are really starting from scratch, which is much easier.

J: On a basic level, it's more fun for people to come away on to a course, and so people are better disposed towards it. It is less likely that people have been made to come to an off-site course. They may have been, but they are more likely to have wanted to come themselves. It's a different kettle of fish.

H: Mostly you are training people to go back into their workplace to train others. How important is this factor of responsibility? It sounds as if people are not that conscious of it while they are on the course. Otherwise wouldn't they demand more attention to the issue of becoming a trainer of their colleagues?

J: We have always said that an important aim of the course is for them to take back what they have learnt to their institution and pass it on, in some way, to their colleagues. But I don't know whether that affects their motivation either way. It comes back to what we were saying earlier about pre-course material. I think people just go along with it, without ever understanding what it means in practice.

H: Does it not create a pressure which motivates them to achieve, maybe more than it motivates them to learn, if you see what I mean?

J: I think it does at the beginning of a course, when I've reminded them of the aims of the course, and they are aware of the expectations on them. Some people are very anxious about it. I'm very quick to reassure them, to remove any element of it being a test of what they've learnt on the course, or of their stamina, or capabilities, or whatever. I'll say to them: 'You only have to do what you feel able to do. Just going back and talking about the course will affect somebody, and if it's only at that level, that's fine'. And I work with them, throughout the course, often on a one-to-one basis, helping them to identify what they think they can do. And helping them prepare to do it.

H: But do they have a clear idea of what the school expects from them after they've been on the course?

J: They know that there is a strong expectation that they'll go back and influence things in their institution as a result of the course. But before they can look at how to be an influence, they need to explore the nature of their role in the institution. That's different from their position. You don't have to be in a powerful position in order to be influential. And likewise, you aren't necessarily influential just because you are a Head of Department. So one of the things that happens on the course is that people reflect on how much influence they have. And they explore new ways of using their influence. So there are two factors operating: what they think they can achieve in the institution (and that relates to how they perceive themselves as part of the institution); and what they want to achieve (which, I think, is related to how much they feel they've changed as a result of the course).

H: Do you provide a structure for that process of reflection and identification of objectives?

J: In a way, it's fundamental to how the course is set up. We insist on more than one person coming from any one institution. They may be two colleagues who don't ever meet in school. They may be the most unlikely combination, it doesn't matter. The fact that there is someone else there from the same institution is a key motivating factor. So the first step is to help people from the same institution to get to know each other, before they even consider what they'll be able to do together after the course. That's probably the most important step, and once that is beginning to happen, then it generates its own motivation, because they recognise that being involved with a colleague means that they are going to be held accountable by that colleague. It means that they will be supporting each other too, of course. But the accountability is usually openly acknowledged and accepted. And it provides a motivation to take more steps than they probably would have felt able to if they'd been on their own.

H: So they jointly define their own objectives, and that will depend on how they relate to each other?

J: Very much so.

H: Do you deal with the issues of on-site/off-site motivation with them? Do you look at the differences between the course they are on with you and the situation they will be going back to?

J: People know that there will be expectations that they will, at the least, disseminate what they have learnt on the course when they are back at work. I know that it's not going to be easy for them. The context they are going back to is completely different to the one in which I'm working with them. But that fact has not always been fully appreciated.

H: By your or by them?

J: By me, I suppose. Although I'm aware of it, I don't think I've given enough thought to that problem. I haven't made it clear enough that they're going to face people who, because they haven't been on the course, aren't going to have the same motivation to learn. I haven't made it clear enough that they've got a much harder job training people back in their institution than I have had in working with them. And when they go back to work after the course, they are often thrown by that situation.

H: Because their expectations are that people will have the same motivation as them?

J: Even though intellectually they know that won't be true. They will say: 'Well, I know my colleagues won't want to know about this — they'll think it's a load of rubbish'. They know that and yet they still get surprised or hurt when they get rejected.

H: Is that because they want to transfer their experience with you, to reproduce it for their colleagues?

J: I think it's something to do with them feeling: 'If only they would open themselves to it they'd learn such a lot'. They know the benefits that they've gained from the course. And they want everybody else to get the same benefits. One of the difficulties is trying to help them to hold back from that.

H: So do they forget their own resistance? They forget how they were at the beginning of the course?

J: Yes, and they get surprised by the resistance of others. They get hurt by it and sometimes they retreat from that, withdraw.

H: Does it make them lose confidence in their own experience?

J: Well, no, it doesn't, and that's the point I've arrived at, really, now, in wondering why it doesn't, because — unless I don't get to hear of people who've just given up without trace — my experience is that people, despite all the knocks and difficulties, carry on. They just keep going.

H: Where does that motivation come from, to carry on?

J: I don't know. I think it's the nature of the work. People do change. And they can't undo that change. So the person going back from a course is different from the one that came. Even if they get nowhere with their colleagues and give up on that, they still persist in putting into practice the things they've learnt. They approach things in a different way and they carry on doing that. And, almost without realising it, that rubs off on other people. Other people perceive that a change has taken place.

Summary

In this chapter we have identified a set of extrinsic factors that influence motivation. We looked at ownership — the degree of control which the learner feels they have over what happens on a course, and suggested that the greater the degree of control, the higher the level of motivation. We explored two factors regarding the content of a course which we feel are crucial to sustained motivation: the content must be perceived by the learner to be relevant to their experience, and to have practical application within that experience. And we stressed two factors regarding the process of the course which can generate a motivational momentum: the learner must have opportunity during the course to 'use' the content both actively, by practising skills, and creatively, by exploring and extending those skills.

Other extrinsic factors that need to be taken into account concern the nature and purpose of the course. If people have been made to attend the course, they may well be predisposed to feel negative or resentful. If the course is in-house, people may feel constrained by their image or role within the organisation. If people are expected to relay their learning from the course when they return to work, they may well feel anxious or unclear about how best to meet those expectations. All these feelings will be blocks to motivation. Giving people the opportunity within the course to explore these issues and articulate their responses to them, can help them to overcome these blocks, and to become motivated to engage in and benefit from the course.

We also identified a set of intrinsic factors, which are outside the control of the trainer. We called these needs, the needs of the learner as a person. There are different levels of need. There are the needs the learner has in relation to the course: not to expose themselves in front of their colleagues would be an example. And there are the generic needs the learner has in relation to group situations: the need to be seen as a powerful or dominating force, for example. These underlying needs have a profound influence on the motivation of the learner. In some cases, there can be a conflict between needs and motivation, where the needs of the learner as an individual undermine or obstruct their motivation to learn.

Activity

Below is a series of questions which you may wish to use to reflect on your responses to the issues we have discussed in this chapter, and the ways in which they relate to your experience as a trainer.

- *What factors influence the motivation of the people who come on your courses?*

Are any of the factors that we identified above influential?
Do other factors apply that are specific to your situation?

- *Do you take steps to affect the motivation of your learners? If so, at what stage in the training process do you intervene*:
  Before the course: if you send out pre-course material, what impact do you think that has on motivation?
  The beginning of the course: do you 'consult' with the learners in order to ensure that the course matches their objectives? If so, what effect do you think this consultation process has on their attitude to the course?
  During the course: do you plan your courses so that they generate and sustain motivation? If so, what strategies do you use?
- *Do you perceive a distinction between motivation and needs?*
  Have there been times when the emotional needs of one or a group of learners have conflicted with their motivation to learn?
  If so, how did you respond to this?

Comment

You may find that motivating the group is a major part of your job as a trainer. They may not want to be there, see no point in being there, resent being there. On the other hand, you may work with groups who are enthusiastic and full of purpose. They are clear about what they want out of the course, and prepared to engage in the process to ensure that they get it. In most situations, the trainer works with both kinds of group. Or, often the most difficult, with groups made up of both kinds of people.

As external trainers working in the public sector, motivating groups has been a prime concern! We have been confident that our material will generate motivation. But we have felt that we needed to take other steps as well. As time went on for both of us, interestingly, those steps became part of the material of the course. Consulting over objectives at the beginning of a course is both a way of ensuring that objectives match, and a way of opening up the issue of power-sharing. Building a contract of ground-rules for the course is both a way of giving the group control over their learning environment, and a way of exploring issues about how people work together.

2 Resistance

People are as likely to be resistant to change as they are to be motivated towards it. In fact they can be both highly motivated and deeply resistant at one and the same time. Few people are continually open to opportunities to learn, develop and change. Such opportunities involve a movement that, however potentially rewarding, is usually experienced as both challenging and disturbing. We believe that one of the functions of the trainer is to create an environment which enables people to overcome their inbuilt resistances to change, which enables them to move.

H: Do you think people come to a course predisposed to be resistant, before they are sure that the course is going to challenge them in any way?

J: I think some people come to a course predisposed to be cynical. That's probably the most common form of resistance that I experience. I'm aware of people at the beginning of a course who sit back in their seats, with a particular expression on their face, and I can tell that they are likely to have this cynicism. It's often a man that's doing this. They will go along with what you are saying, but they are obviously not going to let themselves get engaged by it. I find them quite disturbing to start with. When I suggest that people move and get involved in activities, that person is often the one who's the last to get up, who hangs about on the edge of the group. They give off signals which say: 'Well, now I'm here I might as well go along with it'. They will be drawn into the activity once it gets going, and then afterwards, when we're discussing the exercise, they come out with a high-flown, intellectual question which takes the discussion right away from what happened. I've sometimes got caught out by that.

H: Are there always cynics? Is it part of the dynamic of groups on training courses that they throw up a cynic?

J: It certainly feels like it! Sometimes there are more than one. If I've spotted a cynic on a course, I'll look hard to see if they've got any mates with them. They can have a very powerful influence on the group. If there is more than one, I'll try to ensure that I keep them apart as much as possible. But often all I need to do is go up to them before the course starts and introduce myself, set up some kind of slight personal bond. Or I might make sure that my co-trainer takes that person as a partner for the first exercise in structured conversations.

H: So when you arrive at a venue, do you consciously vet the group for potential resistors?

J: Consciously or unconsciously. I'm open to the signals that people send out. Sometimes I'm wrong — it's literally been a facial expression that I've mis-read, and they haven't been cynical at all. But I know if I'm right because they carry on. They usually want me to see that they are pretty cynical about the whole thing, so they persist with their behaviour. It's a way of getting attention, I think.

H: When you go up to them, do you ever check out your instinct about them? Or challenge them, right out, ask them why they are giving off the signals that they are?

J: No. Partly because I may be wrong. But also, I think it's far too early in a course for that kind of direct challenging. I just go up and smile and introduce myself. I try to disarm them. And sometimes, immediately, they will open up to me, and tell me what's going on for them: 'I didn't really want to be here, you know,' or 'I'm not too keen on all this group therapy stuff'. It's good when that happens, because I know where I stand with them. They've been clear and honest about how they feel, and that provides me with a starting point.

H: How do you reply when they say: 'I'm not into this kind of thing'?

J: It depends on the way that it's said. If it's said very forcefully, I might say: 'Well I'm not sure what you mean by that', and throw it straight back so as to force them to be more explicit about what they think they've come to. If it's said in a fairly mild way, I'll say: 'Well, why don't you give it a go and we'll talk later on and see how you feel then'.

H: And do you make a point of seeking them out to talk about it?

J: I'll make a bee-line for them at the end of that session. It's all part of the disarming process, reassuring them and drawing them into the group. I find that it's easier to engage someone like that on a course where there are people from different schools there, people that they don't know. It makes them a bit less secure in their cynicism. As soon as the course gets going, and they hear what other people are saying, that often dissipates their negativity or their aloofness.

H: How much do you feel it's your responsibility to break that kind of resistance down?

J: I feel it's the responsibility of the whole group. There are times when the resistance is so extreme that I've had to intervene. Once or twice I've suggested that the person leaves, for their sake, as well as for mine and the rest of the course. But I try and do that in a way which will make it easy for them to leave. It's not a confrontation, a show-down. It's more a case of: 'Look, I can see that you feel that this course isn't for you, and you look as if you're not very comfortable with what we're doing. Am I right?' That gives them a chance to say 'yes' or 'no'. And then I say: 'Well, I'd be quite happy if you'd like to leave. If you'd prefer to'. Only on two occasions have they actually left. But that's fine, by me. I don't feel that as a failure or anything.

H: I think most people coming onto a course are not sure what's going to happen to them. But they're probably more concerned about whether it's going to be worth their while, than about whether it's going to challenge them. And it's not always easy to demonstrate the benefit. One of the things that I think helps them to overcome their doubts, or negativity, or cynicism, or anxiety is if they can see me, up-front, as somebody who, at the very least, is going to have energy and give them energy. And that's not a physical energy. I find it hard to describe. I suppose it's to do with being fully there, present, and alive. And that often gets over the first hurdle of suspicion, caution — the potential for resistance. I think it tells people that they are going to have a worthwhile experience, and however difficult, or demanding or risky that experience is, it will also be enjoyable. I know that when I don't feel I've got that energy available, it's much harder to get them going.

J: I think that it's a signal to them that the experience is going to be substantial. And I think people need to know that early on. But once people overcome their initial difficulties and resistances, other factors start to apply. As they become more comfortable with the course, the course becomes more challenging. People respond to the challenges with different degrees of openness. And different forms of resistance emerge. People who apparently feel comfortable with groupwork, for example, who are experienced in it, often stay within their experience rather than push it further. That's a form of resistance. They think that they know what it's all about, and so they think that they've got nothing to learn. But that's just a way of resisting, of not being open. It will often show itself in a slight air of superiority to the rest of the group.

H: Do you find that kind of resistance hard to break down?

J: I can think of one guy who did that and never really changed for the entire time. I really felt that he needed his position to be challenged, but he always found a way of dealing with the challenge. He was a difficult person to handle. He would come up at the end of a session, when I wanted to talk to my colleague, and engage us in conversation about what had happened during the session. He would say things like: 'Well of course, I know what you were trying to do there, and it didn't quite work, did it?'. And in fact, in the practical fieldwork that they did on the course, he was the worst at it, and the people he worked with got very little out of it because of him. I find that form of resistance difficult to handle. And when you've got thirty other people who are taking risks, and you need to support them and help them in it, my feeling is in the end, well, I'll have to leave him where he is.

H: It's not that those kind of people aren't capable. It's that they don't want to go beyond the level they've reached. Because it involves them facing themselves in some way. Which is a shame, because they often have so much potential, if only they could take that step.

J: Sometimes I get the scalpel out and try and open a person up, which is potentially dangerous. Occasionally I've seen that look of hurt bewilderment flit across somebody's face. They don't understand why I'm not colluding with them, or acknowledging that they know what it's all about. I find it a problem. I'm not sure whether I'm being arrogant in taking such a risk; or whether I should leave them where they are. Except that I won't collude with them.

H: I think it's definitely a form of resistance on their part. And that resistance won't be motivated so much by your arrogance as by their need for recognition.

J: Do you think people know what they're doing when they are being resistant in that way?

H: I'm not sure whether they know what they're doing. But I'm sure they don't see what they're doing as a problem, if you see what I mean. I'm sure they don't see it as in any way detrimental, either for themselves, or for the trainer.

J: I think you're right. But I find it hard to believe of those people who resist by thinking that they know it all. I'm sure it is quite a deep-rooted way of protecting themselves, but it feels like they are deliberately blocking. Either by trying to collude with me as an equal. Or with a superiority that says: 'I know all about group-work, and I'm going to go through the motions, but you really can't teach me anything new!'. I find it a bit easier to challenge that form of resistance. Often with a person like that, I'll speak to them individually and put it to them: 'What I'm reading from you is that you've got nothing to learn, am I right?' and 'Oh, no,' will be the answer, 'of course not'. But it usually involves a long discussion to see whether there are any openings where they can show themselves willing to learn. And there usually are. I also try to make it so that other people take them on as well. One of the keys to that is to point out that other people are actually learning. Sometimes I intervene in a small group discussion and say: 'Did you hear what she just said?', because the person has just ridden rough-shod over someone who has made a personal statement about their learning. So by supporting the one who is making the personal statement, I'm also doing the other job of saying: 'Look, you're not hearing that people are learning. Are you learning?'

H: Have you ever experienced resistance from more than one person in the group? Where there's been a hard-core of cynicism or com-placency?

J: I can think of one occasion when I felt the whole course was doing that, bar perhaps one or two individuals! I think it was something to do with the culture of the area where the course was taking place. It was a suburban area, where the schools were mostly well-maintained and well-supported by parents. And there was this incredible complacency in the group. Nobody felt any need to change at all. They were quite happy to be there. But the idea that they review their ways of working, yet alone change them, was a total non-starter. They just couldn't see why they should. They were very nice people. They just went through the motions, that's all.

H: When did you become aware of this?

J: I knew almost from the start that there was something wrong, although I didn't think of it as resistance at the time. But I knew that I wasn't getting through. And I puzzled and puzzled about it, and that night I couldn't sleep for thinking about how I was going to get through to them. It got to about mid-day of the next day before I wound myself up to challenge them. I took a deep breath and told them that I was feeling as if I was wasting my time here. I said: 'We're having a good time, but nobody's learning anything from it, and I feel, at this moment, that we might as well all pack up and go home. What do you think?' There was a stunned silence, and one or two smiles and smirks. But I stuck to my guns and just let the silence go until somebody said something. And then we spent the next two hours talking about why. Why they were there and what they were supposed to be doing. We went back to the principles and objectives that I'd explained at the beginning of the course. I remember saying: 'You just went through the motions, didn't you? You went through the motions of saying "We agree to those objectives. We understand these principles". And you've been going through the motions ever since, haven't you?'.

H: Were you worried about being put into some kind of teacher position, where you were having to tell them off for misbehaving?

J: It would have been so easy to do with that group — they were like naughty children. It was a struggle not to. But I was more interested in looking at what the problem was. And I recognised that part of the problem was that I hadn't done my homework well enough beforehand. So I didn't understand where they were coming from. I don't quite know how I would have tackled it any differently. But I had definitely misunderstood the culture of the course. I wasn't structuring it so that it met their needs. And in a way I was going through the motions just as much as they were. I should have challenged them early on. Because when I did, they were open about what they wanted, what their needs were, in a way that they hadn't been before. And what transpired was that this particular group felt very under-valued by the system they worked in. I think they really wanted an opportunity to express their resentment.

H: It's interesting that on the one hand they are complacent, and on the other they are dissatisfied. It's almost a contradiction. The real problem is their dissatisfaction with the status they have within their institutions. But they relay that to you in the form of complacency and lack of openness. I'm never sure whether complacency is the problem, or whether it's a misleading expression of the real problem.

J: Interestingly enough, the feedback at the end was that it had been a great course. And I'm sure that's partly because of the turbulence that occurred on the second afternoon. The course had given them an opportunity to own their dissatisfaction, share it with others, and find out that they weren't alone. They each made a plan of what they were going to do when they went back after the course. I went back the next month to run the second part of the course as arranged. And almost to a person they said they hadn't been able to do anything because of how things were in their institutions, but that the course had been marvellous for themselves personally. I just didn't believe them, because they'd allowed themselves to be swallowed up again by the system. They'd done nothing, and they'd changed nothing.

H: It was probably marvellous because they'd had a chance to express their negativity. They'd got things off their chest. They don't sound like they were committed to changing anything. Sounds like they are happy to be dissatisfied. Better that than take any responsibility for the situation. I come across quite a few people like that in local authorities. And they are generally difficult to work with. I set up a ground-rule at the beginning of the course which says: 'No excuses'! Otherwise they spend half the time blaming their senior management. I've come to think that there's a general rule that people who don't feel valued, won't value what you do.

J: It seems to stand to reason somehow. I can think of a number of individuals where the root of their resistance is their feeling of not being valued. But they are really saying that they don't value themselves.

H: There was a woman on a course that I ran who seemed to me to be comfortable only when she felt inadequate in relation to other members of the group. She would continually say: 'Oh, it's all right for them, they've got a lot of experience, but I haven't'. There was a resistance there which wasn't critical of me, or the material, or anything. It was critical of herself. It was her way of not engaging, of not taking the risk of engaging and finding out what her capabilities or strengths were. Of all the forms of resistance I've come across, that is the one I've found hardest to deal with. I didn't know how to work with her. I knew she was frightened of me, but I don't think I was threatening her as much as threatening the position she'd constructed of being inadequate.

J: I think one of the big factors in engaging people and getting them to want to change, is the demonstration that everybody is valued.

However resistant, unpleasant, challenging and hostile they may be! The process of valuing everyone's contribution is central to what we do. When people see that this is what we are doing, it is a great step towards insight into what the work is about. People have said to me: 'Where do you get your patience from?'. And it *is* about patience. It's about challenging people, but in a way that is essentially valuing of them. And it's about never putting anyone down.

H: That's certainly one of the guiding principles behind my work. But some people don't want to be valued. I feel like they put a pressure on me to undervalue them to confirm their own sense of lack of self-worth. It's like a downward spiral, which I find difficult to get out of. There was a guy, I remember, part of a small course, maybe ten people. And he locked me into a similar kind of spiral. He put an enormous amount of energy into showing that he was above the rest of the group and that he really had nothing to learn from the course. He left himself no time for reflection, or for self-awareness, no time to just be open to what was happening. He seemed determined to use the course as a way of feeding his vanity.

J: Is that different from him undervaluing himself?

H: I think that resistance is a strategy by which people won't take the risks they need to take. Because if they took them, it is likely they would feel better about themselves in some way. I felt, in his case, that, somewhere along the line, in his life, his needs for recognition were not being met, and that this was really getting in his way. He was continually looking for recognition in inappropriate places. Like the course. And the pity of it was that not only was the course not going to give him the kind of recognition he was looking for, but also his behaviour stopped him from getting other kinds of recognition which would have nourished him.

J: I do exactly connect with what you're saying. I can think of several times when things have happened like that.

H: It's hard, because you either have to challenge them to the point where they open up, or you have to leave them alone, and challenging can be risky because it is potentially hurtful. I felt that if he were to move, he would have to go through quite a growth experience to get out of the set he'd got himself into. I spent a lot of time on that course working out how much I was prepared to give him. And also working out what my motivation would be for doing it, and how much I was prepared to take up any consequences that might arise. In the end I decided not to do anything.

I didn't feel generous enough, in relation to him, to trust myself. Nor did I feel there was sufficient time for it to be safe and effective. And I didn't feel that I wanted to invest that amount of emotional energy in him.

J: I think that understanding your own motivations is crucial. I have felt that form of resistance from a certain type of person. It is often to do with me being a woman, and it often comes from another woman. I think it's something to do with them undervaluing themselves, and not accepting that another woman could be doing an upfront, high-focus job, like being a trainer. I remember one woman, who had been incredibly difficult throughout the course, both in open challenge and covert resistance. One evening, it was as if she came in for the kill! She took me off into a corner, away from everyone else, because she wanted to talk with me. And she used all sorts of strategies for not talking about what was really at stake. Which was how I, a woman, had arrived at the position that I was in, that she perceived me being in. She engaged my attention, I allowed myself to be engaged by her, for the entire evening, telling anecdotes about her situation at work. I felt she was trying to tell me things about herself, and maybe ask for some advice about the situation she was describing, but she did it so obliquely, and she rejected anything that I said, any advice I offered. She prevented me from sitting and talking with any of the other people on the course. I look back on that as a failing: not recognising what was going on, and allowing myself to be drawn in by her. I allowed it to happen, I think, because I had a kind of compulsion to be respected by this woman for what I was doing. And also a compulsion to make her see that she could do it too. She was aggressive and that put me on the defensive. But I didn't see it coming. I learned from that experience. The next time I thought it was going to happen (again it was a woman) I anticipated it. My strategy in that instance was to award the woman a lot of status. I felt it was important for me to go to her and disarm her, rather than let her undermine me.

H: That is always my strategy now: to try and give people the recognition they need, as early as possible. I try and meet their emotional needs before they become a block, and develop into a form of resistance. But there are times when I can't do that, when their needs are too great. The other kind of resistance I come across is a more intellectual one, where people resist by disagreeing on an ideological level. They argue with the rationale behind the work.

When people react to an activity, or a discussion, or a piece of direct teaching by wanting to argue about the implicit values or ideology behind it, I am now very much on my guard. Sometimes it's straightforward. But I tend to perceive their action as a form of resistance. I think that they'd rather talk about it in the abstract than experience it for real.

J: Especially if what they are being asked to do is uncomfortable for them, if they find it disturbing or feel threatened by it in some way. It's as if they retreat into the abstract. And they can tie things up in complex discussion for quite a long time in order to deflect things away from what might be uncomfortable.

H: It's very hard to side-step that, because it can seem as if you are being dismissive. In the end, what I say to people is: 'That's very interesting, but I don't think it's that useful at the moment. I think it would be more useful for you, now, to do the activity'. But they will often persist in trying to prove that they are right, even when I'm not saying that they're wrong!

J: I'll also say something like: 'I'll talk about that with you later, in a break, if you like, but at the moment it's holding everybody else up', just to make them aware of the other people, and what's happening to them. But they put a lot of energy into maintaining their position.

H: The energy they put into it is a clear tip-off to me about how uncomfortable they feel with the activity. I often get the sense that when people are striving to make ideological sense of what's happening, when they are trying to assimilate their experiences into some value-structure, they are not fully open to the whole experience. They are only absorbing the parts that fit easily, that they can readily make sense of. They want to endorse what they already believe in. They're not that interested in change. Or rather, they're not that interested in changing! It's an intellectual or political concept. It doesn't apply to them personally!

J: Do you find that people want you to declare your position, make some kind of statement about the values behind your work?

H: That sometimes happens, not necessarily in a challenging way. But I tend to steer clear of making such statements. Not because I don't want to expose my rationale for what I do, but because it can get in the way of people developing their own. When I experience that pressure to make clear statements of rationale, I tend to check out whether it is in fact a way of people resisting the need to sort out their own understanding of the values behind the work. If it comes from me, there's a danger that they will just borrow it, carry it away in their suitcase at the end of the course. And then I'm not sure how useful it is. If it hasn't been generated from their experience, I'm not sure how usable it is.

J: This strikes so many chords for me. There was a year when a researcher was evaluating the effects of in-service training in Active Tutorial Work. And we had these debates about a rationale or theoretical framework for the work. Every time he talked to groups of people that had been on our courses, that was the thing that came up. Even with people who had gone a long way down the road through various levels of training and were now training other teachers. They would say to him: 'I'd like more theoretical framework'. And he would bring that to us, as if to say, 'Well, here you are, here's some feedback, maybe you should think about this'. I used to have endless arguments with him. I'd say: 'Well, what is it they're actually asking for, what is it? Is it about why groupwork works? Or is it about why they like it themselves and have taken it on board? Is it a learning theory or what? I don't understand what they're asking for when they say, 'we want a more theoretical framework'. He said he used to feel they were asking for a bit of all of that, but particularly about the rationale that underpinned it. And I used to say: 'What's the use of me saying this is the theoretical framework behind Active Tutorial Work? So that they can then go back to their schools, and say: "Jill Baldwin says it's this"? It's got to come from them. They've got to understand it for themselves and be able to find the words to say it for themselves'.

H: As you were talking, I was thinking about why people want it. What do they need, here? And what I understand from what you were saying is that they need an endorsement of their experience because they're unsure of it for themselves. They are unsure of it because it's so individualised, so they want to make sure that their individualised experience is located within an external set of values. They want to make sure they are not alone. I think it can be alarming for people if they've been through quite a deep, experiential process on a course. There's a rawness about new perception and new self-awareness and new awareness of others. They are confronted by a challenge, which is whether to continue along that route, to face the implications of these new perceptions, or to ignore them once they get back to normality. Their experience on the course has been about change, about them changing.

And a ready-made theoretical or ideological framework which endorses that may well provide some security. But I suspect that sometimes it's wanted as an excuse for not continuing the process of change. They want to be sure that they've arrived in the right place rather than that they're in a process which they have to take responsibility for continuing for themselves.

Summary

In the last chapter we looked at the issue of motivation. In this chapter we focused on what can be regarded as the opposite: resistance. At one point we defined resistance as a 'strategy by which people avoid taking the risks they need to take'. It is a way of holding back, of not learning or developing, of staying still. It is also a natural response to challenge, and as such, part of the dynamic of learning.

We identified a number of forms in which resistance can manifest itself: cynicism about the learning process; scepticism about the value or substance of the content of a course; collusion with the trainer to indicate parity; display of superiority; argument about ideology or rationale. We explored some of the reasons why people are resistant: because they don't want to move outside what they know; because they undervalue themselves, and therefore their potential to develop; because they feel undervalued, and see no benefit in self-development.

Activity

Below are a series of questions which you may wish to use to reflect on your responses to the issues we have discussed in this chapter, and the ways in which they relate to your experience as a trainer.

- *Are there factors inherent in your situation that give rise to resistance amongst the people you train?*
  For example: the attitude to training within the organisation? the kind of people you train? the content or process of your training courses? the kind of trainer that you are?
- *If these, or other, factors do lead to resistance, are there ways in which you can affect or influence them to minimise the likelihood of resistance?*

- *If you do experience resistance, do you come across particular forms of resistance?*
  Do you, for example, recognise the forms of resistance that we have talked about in this chapter?
  Do you come across other forms of resistance?
- *How do you deal with resistance?*
  It may not be appropriate for you to think about this question in a general way. It may be more useful to look at specific incidents that come to mind, and see if there are aspects of the way you handled those situations which apply more generally to your responses to resistance.

Comment

As in the last chapter, different trainers will come across different degrees of resistance to their work, depending on the situation they are working in. If a group of people is not motivated, it is likely that they will be resistant in one form or another. Whatever their situation, most trainers will have experience of resistant learners. Most of the trainers we have met have come up with horror stories about such people at the drop of a hat! And they, like us, have found resistance a remarkably difficult phenomenon.

Generating motivation at the beginning of a course will in most cases overcome people's initial resistance. Some people carry their resistance beyond that point. Others become resistant when they are challenged at a particular point in the course. Identifying resistance early enables you to disarm scepticism before it develops into resistance. But more deep-rooted resistance can be quite intractable. Challenging it can result in you being dragged into a dialogue which excludes the rest of the group, or in hurt withdrawal by the 'resistor'.

In general we felt that resistance was closely linked to value and self-worth. If people feel valued, they have a more secure platform from which to take risks. They will also be surer that they will gain recognition for taking those risks, or meeting challenges. If people value themselves, they will value their own learning and development, and perceive it as increasing their value. People with low self-esteem are often more concerned to preserve that self-image than to challenge it. In some cases, all the trainer can do is promote the sense that they value everybody in the group equally, and hope that that will have some positive effect.

3 Confrontation and conflict

There are times when resistance is not always expressed directly. It is often more an undercurrent that can be sensed, and which has a subtle, intangible impact on a course. There are times, however, when resistance spills out onto the surface, often as a direct attempt to undermine the course, either by stopping it in its tracks, or by hijacking it in different directions. In such cases, when the resistance is active and directive, we call it confrontation. Sometimes the learner will confront the trainer, challenging their credibility, or the credibility of their material. At other times, the learner may channel their resistance into conflict with other participants on the course.

J: I remember talking about this in the chapter on Power and Authority: the effect of a direct challenge on my sense of authority. About the value of being prepared to show your vulnerability so that people see it as a strength and not a weakness. That's very effective with the whole group, and often they will take on the challenge with me and it will be a significant point in the group's development. But it won't always meet the needs of the challenger. They may keep going on, or fall sullenly silent. If that's the case, I will offer to speak with them privately during a break. I try not to get locked into a dialogue with them, which is often what they want. And they can make it very difficult for me to extract myself from that dialogue.

H: I'm always tempted to try and deal with the challenge there and then. To resolve it in some way. But often they don't want their problem to be resolved. They seem to get hooked on the confrontation. And the longer I get trapped in those dialogues, the harder it is to find a way out of them. I try to bring other people into the conversation, but sometimes they just don't want to get involved.

There's a balance between meeting the needs of the challenger and meeting the needs of the rest of the group. The group has to know that you are taking their needs into account too. I try to validate the person's point of view, without agreeing with it. If they persist, I will defer the conversation until later. Often when I go back to people and say: 'Do you want to talk about that now?' they won't want to, the need isn't there any longer. Which makes me think that it's often not the issue that's at stake — there's something else going on.

J: It's much harder when there is more than one person out there, a hard core of people who are throwing up a block of some kind. It's harder to know quite what is going on, who's saying what and why. It can generate an unpleasant atmosphere of aggression or rebellion.

H: I had an experience like that when I was running a course for trainers. Right at the beginning a small group of them brought up this point about how people wouldn't come to training courses unless they got a qualification at the end of it. So why bother with a course like this? Really it was a pointless conversation. The fact was that there were no qualifications for the kind of training that they were involved in. But it created a very unpleasant mood at the start of the course, and I found it very difficult to deal with. What I did was to hand it over to them as a group. I said: 'Maybe what you need to look at is whether you want to be here, given that we're not going to deal with that issue. But the more time you take deciding, the less time we will have to work on things that we can actually do something about'. I tried to give them power in the situation to decide how they could best use the time as a group. And then I just left it with them and they said: 'No, you're right, we'll leave it alone'. I felt that the content of the confrontation wasn't important. It was so obviously something that was outside the scope of the course. What was important was the confrontation. It was an attempt to hijack the course. It took me some time to realise that, and then I decided to step out of it. I made my position clear, but knew that the longer I went on arguing my case, the longer the argument would go on. I thought if I took myself out of the frame, the issue wouldn't seem that important. It worked, but it was a bit high-risk. And it didn't clear the atmosphere at all.

J: There are times when a confrontation like that can be a turning point for a course in terms of shifting the power towards the group. But that generally only happens on longer courses, rarely on the one- or two-day courses that I've run. Certainly on a five-day residential there is a moment when there's quite a lot of turbulence in the room and the challenge comes out of that turbulence. There are times when I actively look for it. I know it's got to come at some time and I want it to, because I want to hand over power to the group. It's the point when I feel that people are ready to take on power in the situation, when they are ready to stop seeing me as the person with all the power. I do what you just said, I step out of the frame, so that they can't channel all this energy into confrontation with their authority-figure, so that they start using it themselves, for their own benefit. With me out of the frame, they do start to use it positively, not as confrontation. And that is the turning point for the course.

H: But it is dangerous to do that too early, because if they are not ready, they may misuse the power, make the wrong decisions, or not take everybody into account. If it happens too early, they see it as me avoiding my responsibility as the trainer. That's what happened on that course, I think, which is why, although they made the right decision in the end, the atmosphere stayed churlish for a while.

J: I think the strategy of keeping out of the dialogue is sound, though. When I'm training trainers, I advise them to leave a silence if they are challenged or confronted by anybody, to delay responding just a little bit longer than is comfortable. More often than not, somebody will take it up for you. They'll shift the focus away from you, and the group will start dealing with the challenge. But I don't present that to them as a way of avoiding conflict. It is a very simple way of shifting the locus of power in the room. It is one of the ways in which the group learns that the trainer hasn't got all the answers, and that they are capable of generating answers for themselves.

H: For me, it still comes down to the point in the course when it happens. Last week I had somebody, when people were giving their expectations of the course, who said: 'Well, I was coming along to see how many people turn up to these training courses because my impression is actually that it's pathetic and hardly anyone turns up and it's a waste of time'. It wasn't hard to leave a silence after that one because it quite threw me, I couldn't work out what he was really saying behind that. So I left a silence, and nobody said anything, because they were all as thrown as I was, I think.

J: It's quite an oblique challenge, isn't it? As if he was trying to detach himself from what was going on, and not be part of it.

H: He was actually sitting apart from everybody else as well. I didn't think it was enough just to leave it and go on to the next person. So I said, 'Well, what do you think of this turn-out?'. I wanted to try and bring him into the group a bit, otherwise he'd have stayed on the outside all day. And he said: 'It's pretty good'. And I said: 'Oh good, well let's see how it goes then'. Then I moved on, and didn't give him any more space, didn't try and do too much, just left him with it, and left the group with it. It was difficult, that, because I wanted to do more, I wanted him to show his commitment to the course and to the other people. But I wouldn't have been able to do it at that point. And maybe it's more important not to try, to let it go, and let the other person take responsibility, rather than see it as my responsibility to do something about it. It wasn't until the end that he finally became part of the group, and sat in a semi-circle with everybody else.

J: That kind of confrontation is so much to do with getting attention. Maybe all kinds of confronation are. You have to evaluate whether to give people the attention or not. I think it's very rarely worth it. There's a man I'm thinking of who throughout a one-week course was confronting me all the time with his need for attention. Your story reminded me of him because he started at the point when people were stating their expectations. He was the only person on the course who worked with handicapped children, and so his needs and perceptions were quite different. I had to say to him: 'Well, you've had a programme circulated with the aims and objectives of the course, from what you saw on that, do you think those hopes and expectations are going to be met?' and he said, 'I'm used to getting what I can from courses because there's never any courses which are exactly designed for me'.

H: That's another oblique challenge. It's hard to know who he's getting at. It sounds like he'd rather not get what he says he wants!

J: I tried to deal with it then and there, at some length, actually. And I think maybe I gave him too much attention early on. It set a precedent, and from then on he felt justified, in this slightly fatalistic way, to keep asking these questions which were complete red herrings. He wasn't being aggressive. In fact he was a really charming man, which made it far harder to deal with. By the middle of the week, whenever he did this, the whole of the room would go silent. Not out of respect. It was a completely dismissive silence.

H: Do you think, by giving attention to the problem right at the beginning, that you endorsed it, at least in his eyes? It sounds as if you gave him licence to stay put, rather than try to move towards belonging to the course.

J: We tried to compensate for the mismatch between his needs and what the course was offering by giving him the space to say what he wanted. But he kept misusing the space. And all that did was reinforce his feelings that nobody wanted to know about his problems, because he kept inserting them into the course at times when people didn't want to listen to him. He was setting himself up as the victim all the time. It became a self-fulfilling prophecy. I think he'd have succeeded in doing that whatever we'd done, to be honest. I think he'd have found ways of brandishing his dissatisfaction. But what I was doing patently didn't work, because at the end of the course, he did challenge me quite directly, very confrontationally. People were planning what action to take when they went back into their schools, and he suddenly burst out: 'Why don't you just tell us what to do? Why do we have to re-invent the wheel? You must know by now what works and what doesn't. Why don't you just tell us what to do?' And it was clear, in spite of all my efforts, that I hadn't made any impact on him whatsoever.

H: One of the exercises I use sometimes when people are being very negative, is to ask them to turn their statements into demands. I wonder whether that would have helped with him? He was making statements about not getting his needs met by the course, but if he could have turned them into demands that he could make of you, or of other people, that might have shifted him out of the negative into the positive. The work for him is to make it a demand that you can meet. I use it as an exercise when people are moaning a lot — usually about senior management in local authorities, and I'll say: 'Ok, turn that complaint into a demand'. And they'll come up with something quite unrealistic like: 'I want you to resign' or something, and I'll say: 'Ok, now try making a demand that the other person is going to be able to do something about, a realistic demand'. They're usually very resistant to doing that, because it involves doing something positive about the situation. But at some point they see: 'Ah, maybe I do have some power here, maybe I can do something about this situation'. It sounds like the same kind of thing with this guy. If he could make demands of the group that were in their power to meet, maybe that would be just enough to shift him out of his destructive cycle.

J: If that was done as a group exercise too, so that it wasn't just him doing it, that could work quite well. It's true in teaching too. There are always people who are locked in the negative. I get very affected by it sometimes. I remember once, when I was introducing a course, a woman was so obviously switched off from what I was saying. She kept turning her head and looking to see who else was in the room, all the time. And I found it a real struggle just to keep talking.

H: And this was because she was being negative? Did she continue like that through the course?

J: She disrupted every group she was in in some way, usually by trivialising what we were doing and making comments which distracted other people. And because they were colleagues of hers, they allowed it and went along with it. They didn't challenge her. But she was making me more and more annoyed and after a while my co-trainer said to me: 'It's showing on your face, Jill'. By this time, I was getting really angry because every time I wanted them to stop and listen to me, she carried on talking, just loud enough for it to affect the people near her.

H: I think that behaviour is so aggressive. And I'm sure if you said that to her, or said: 'Do you realise how confrontational you are being?' she would be amazed.

J: Several times I paused deliberately, and looked at her, trying to make the point, but she still persisted. She ignored my messages. My colleague was becoming anxious about what was going to happen and how it would be resolved. Her non-verbal signals were telling me: 'You're not handling this right'. It was clearly showing so much that I was angry, and I think it's counter-productive to show how rattled I am. So I changed tack completely. I'd overheard something dismissive that she'd said in her small group, and the next time I stopped to speak to the full group, I referred to what I had heard her say, addressing myself directly to her: 'It's what you were saying, in your group, isn't it? That this could easily be seen as a waste of time'. She was totally taken aback. Partly because she realised that I'd overheard what she'd been saying. But mainly because I was taking notice of it, and using it to reinforce what I was saying. And from that point, she gradually changed her behaviour for the rest of the day.

H: Is there a principle there, in terms of dealing with that kind of confrontation?

J: I'd been going along the track of trying to make an example of her because I'd got angry about her behaviour; and that was completely wrong in that situation. I suppose it might work at other times. But for her, I was just reinforcing her feelings of being outside the group. I was lucky that my colleague tipped me off. Because I was getting so angry that I was losing perspective. The strength of my feeling was getting in the way. And that's certainly something I've learnt to try to be aware of: the point where my irritation starts feeding the problem, so that it gets bigger. The real problem was this woman's feeling of exclusion. And the solution was to find a way of including her, helping her to feel included. I was focusing on her behaviour, not her problem.

H: Do you think there are times when that 'including' strategy isn't appropriate?

J: There are times when people are just rude or inconsiderate, where it's enough to just pause to make the point that they are interrupting me or making my job difficult, or holding up the group. I'll pause just long enough for it to be uncomfortable, and often that will be enough. People will understand what I'm doing, and adjust accordingly. This woman required a lot more effort.

H: How did you deal with her after that point?

J: I went and sat with her small group for a while. And she said: 'Oh, we've got Miss here' and that kind of thing. I gently ignored that and just kept on plugging away at getting her to feel part of what was going on, getting her to see that it could be of value to her. I kept asking for her opinion on what other people were saying, bringing her in to their discussion really. At one point she went from one extreme to the other, and she started taking over and speaking for everybody. So then I had to gently say: 'Are you speaking for the whole group or are you just speaking for yourself?'. And I brought the rest of the group in, challenging her statement and disagreeing with her. Finally I got her and her group to work together. But it was a slow process.

H: Do you ever get situations on your courses where there is conflict between participants? It sounds like that could have happened in the group you have just described. If I'd been in that group, I think I would have confronted that woman about her behaviour.

J: There are certain activities on our courses which generate turbulence. They are activities which depend on people working together, usually having to go out of the course and into a real-world situation to complete a task together. Part of the activity is them learning to work together and support each other. It's always a difficult, challenging activity, but then it's very rewarding and people get a lot out of it, and learn a lot from it. But occasionally, where two people are completely opposite in their values, and attitudes and beliefs, and can't find a way to come to terms with that, the activity will lead to conflict between the pair or the group. And then the conflict is escalated by the pressure of time running out.

H: You insist on them having to go out and do the task?

J: There are other teachers, or perhaps a group of parents or a class of children, who are waiting for them to come and work with them, so they've got to do it, and they've got to find some way of working together. There's usually a practical solution, where they each take responsibility for separate parts of the task, and they'll accept that solution. There was one occasion, with a man and a woman working together, and the woman just burst into tears. She was so anxious about the task and he was so obdurate about how it should be done. She just didn't believe it would work, and they were getting nowhere. I had to go and sit with them and help them plan, but also I had to point out to the man: 'Do you realise that you've actually reduced your partner to tears?'.

H: In those situations, do you ever make connections between how the person was being on the course and how they are in real life?

J: Not at that point. It's unusual for me to be so directly challenging of a person at any point on a course. But that kind of challenge often happens when people come back from their tasks. They debrief their experiences in a group which we call a support group, which meets regularly at key points during the course. And sometimes the support groups break down. They have got to a point where people are quite challenging of each other within the group, and sometimes things start to go wrong, or get out of hand. They don't seem to have the resources within the group to get themselves through it. And there will be open conflict between people.

H: Do you leave them to find ways of resolving that conflict together, or do you intervene at that point?

J: I keep a careful watch when the support groups are operating. If I felt things had got to a point which couldn't be resolved by the group — there have been times when people have wanted to leave the course, for example — I'd move in and at least make sure that everybody's perceptions of what happened are heard, really as the starting point for rebuilding the group. It can take a long time to resolve.

H: Do you see that kind of conflict as necessary to the learning process? Is it an indication of a commitment and openness that you regard as necessary prerequisites to a person's or group's development?

J: It's certainly true that people can learn a lot from those conflict situations, and at quite a deep, personal level. But it's a level which often exceeds the declared parameters of the course. I don't try to create conflict within groups. But I recognise that if it happens, it can be channelled creatively. And it can profoundly affect people.

H: There have certainly been times when I've felt a group needed to be more challenging of itself, where conflict could have played a useful part in making that happen. There are times when I know that there is underlying conflict in the group, but it's being kept under the surface. I would prefer it to come out into the open so that it can be dealt with, rather than generate this unpleasant undercurrent. I'll take steps to try and make that happen sometimes. There was a guy on one course who was being very dominating, a bully really. Everybody else put up with it, but they were clearly not happy about it. I paired this man off in one activity with someone who I thought might challenge him. And in the end the partner just pulled out of the activity and let the guy do it. Which he did without a backward glance. People started coming up to me in breaks and complaining about him. And I thought, the real learning here, for all of us, is learning how to deal with this man.

J: I'm not sure that I would draw that to the surface unless I had to. But I think I would certainly have gone up to your man after the activity and asked him how he felt about the fact that he hadn't been able to complete a paired activity with his partner.

H: He felt fine about it. He didn't see it as a problem at all. I stepped back at that point because I felt he needed challenging to a degree that I didn't want to take on. And I think the group felt the same, which was a shame. I tried to give him some hard feedback at certain points during the course, by telling him how he affected me by the way he did some of the activities. Partly so he could get a sense of the effect he was having, and partly to create an opportunity for other people to tell him how they felt about him. But he was really good at receiving feedback. It didn't seem to have any impact on him at all!

J: I sometimes will challenge what I call the cosiness of a group, where they get to a stage when they feel that everything's wonderful, and they're only operating at a certain level, and I can see that they're unaware of or avoiding underlying themes. I watch for a point where I can go in and take that layer off for them, even to the point of saying: 'Well, don't you think this is all very cosy?' and the response is usually: 'What do you mean?' And I'll give an example where somebody was put down and let it go. Often the group will defend themselves against me, and resist my intervention, and I'll have to work hard to get them to see that they are now ready to move on to another level of openness and supportiveness.

H: I always find that the crunch level is the communication of negative feelings. That's always a hurdle: either people don't do it, and then the feelings accumulate and get out of control. Or someone does it badly and causes conflict or hurt of some kind.

J: I think there's a lot of truth in that. It may depend on the size of the group. Small groups seem to be under greater pressure. Groups of six or seven seem better able to sustain being supportive without generating negativity. But maybe it's just that it takes longer. Or they can mask the tension more easily because there are more of them. Do you have ways in which you help people to express their negativity?

H: It's not always appropriate for me to intervene, but if it is, I use a technique which I call 'the round'. That provides a structure where each person can speak in turn, without interruption for an agreed amount of time. When they have finished, the next person speaks, but can't comment on what the preceding people have said in their turn. It gives people a clear, secure space to talk about their feelings. And it encourages people to listen to everybody in the group, and to hear what they have got to say. It's the start of a process, but often people are so surprised by the effect of doing a round, that it will shift the dynamic completely. It can throw people into the next level of openness. It can very quickly generate a respectful and caring atmosphere.

J: Would you do a round with a really big group?

H: It's best with no more than eight or nine people in a round. But I've split big groups up if there are small rooms available so that each round can have its own space. When I work with teams I suggest that they use the round as a way of starting or finishing their meetings. But it is especially useful for helping people keep up-to-date with their negative feelings, because it provides a semi-formal structure in which people are relatively safe to say what they want. It may take time for people to take real risks, but the round can provide a safe arena for them to do so.

J: Going back to the group you were talking about earlier, with the guy who was so difficult to work with. Did you use the round there? Did you use it as a way of uncovering what was going on?

H: No I didn't. Maybe I should have, I don't know. At the time it felt too big, and I was feeling so antagonistic towards him that I didn't quite trust myself. It would have meant interrupting the whole programme. And my fear was that it could have taken over. People didn't want to take him on, and I didn't want to create the situation where they felt they had to. Maybe I was just copping out, I don't know. Have you been in a similar position?

J: I've seen groups in what looks like dead-lock, where they are getting very, very ratty with each other, and it didn't look like it was going to get better. I've intervened in those situations. I'll pull up a chair and ask if I can join in. That often has the effect of breaking it, because they'll know why you've joined them, and that sometimes releases somebody to say: 'We're not getting on very well here'. And that allows me to say: 'Well, do you want to talk about it? What's the problem?'. But I don't think I would bring things to the surface unless I felt sure that I was going to be able to help resolve things when they came out into the open. That has to be the guiding rule. You can't do everything. And it's as much their responsibility as it is yours. Sometimes you have to let things go.

Summary

In this chapter, we have explored different forms of confrontation that can occur on training courses. If the nature of a course is challenging, it is likely that it will generate turbulence within groups or individuals. This, in turn, can lead to some form of confrontation. Confrontation is usually an active form of resistance, an aggressive expression of anxiety or resentment.

Sometimes this is directed at the trainer who is seen as the cause of the turbulence, or as an authority-figure to be resisted. In our experience, the content of a confrontation is less significant than its function, which is often an attempt to disrupt the course, either by invalidating it or redirecting it. Focusing on the content can lead to tortuous and fruitless dialogue which does nothing to resolve the conflict, and often feeds it by increasing misunderstanding and irritability.

The point when someone confronts the trainer is usually the worst time to attempt resolution. The learner's emotions are high, and their position at its most entrenched. Accepting their point of view and bringing other members of the group into the dialogue can help to defuse the situation and divert focus away from the trainer. Confrontation often serves to reinforce a learner's feeling of exclusion from the group or from the course. Giving them too much attention at the point of challenge, so that they become a special case, a problem, can endorse those feelings. Often their real need will be to feel included.

Sometimes confrontation occurs between participants on a course. If the group is working in pairs or in small groups, tension can be generated by differences in approach to the activity or to groupwork generally. Groups can often manage such internal conflict themselves, and learn much from doing so. But there are times when the conflict becomes unmanageable, and the trainer needs to intervene. There may also be times when the trainer feels that a group needs to experience some turbulence in order to develop further, to move to a new level of openness or insight.

Activity

Below are a series of questions which you may wish to use to reflect on your responses to the issues we have discussed in this chapter, and the ways in which they relate to your experience as a trainer.

- *Do you get confrontation on your training courses?*
  If so, what form does it take? For example: is confrontation directed against you or other trainers on the course? Is there tension or conflict between participants? Or does the confrontation take another form?

What causes the confrontation? For example, is it caused by misunderstanding about the purpose or the content of the course? . . . the nature of the training process or antagonism to training generally? . . . personality clashes? Or are there other causes?

- *What is your attitude to confrontation on training courses?*
  Do you see it as integral to the learning process — to be encouraged?
  Do you see it as an interruption of the learning process — to be avoided?

- *How do you deal with confrontation if it occurs?*
  This will depend on the causes and nature of the confrontation, but in general, do you: attempt to resolve the confrontation yourself? attempt to keep out of the confrontation, whether it is directed at you, or at other learners within the group? involve other members of the course in the confrontation, if they are not involved already? use the confrontation as the basis for learning, providing a structure for the group to explore possible resolutions? have other ways in which you deal with confrontation?

Comment

The frequency with which confrontation of any kind occurs on your courses will depend on the kind of training you are involved in, and the kind of people you train. Some trainers use conflict deliberately to achieve particular learning objectives. Some will be used to drawing the flak, for example in organisations where people are very anti-training. Others will avoid confrontation wherever possible as it will obstruct learning, and will work in situations where conflict of any kind is rare. Most trainers, however, will have experienced confrontation directed at themselves at some time in their career.

People will develop different strategies for dealing with confrontation depending on their attitude to it. Some may exert their power of position to stop confrontation quickly. Some may want to resolve conflict to the satisfaction of the people involved before the course progresses any further. Some may involve the group in a structured or unstructured way. Most trainers will have a range of strategies for dealing with the different situations that arise.

In general, we regard confrontation as an expression of some form of need. We may or may not be able to meet that need, depending on the objectives of the course, and our own capacity for taking it on. There are situations where we will defer conflict to a later time, because it is irrelevant to the needs of the rest of the group. If we feel that the whole group can contribute to the resolution of the problem, and that it would be useful for them to do so, we will look for ways of including them. This may mean bringing them into a fraught exchange. It may mean stopping the course and proposing a process for resolving the conflict. Such a process needs to be managed so that people have an opportunity to reflect on what they have learnt, and to express their feelings about what has happened. The trainer needs to ensure that the potential for learning is maximised, and that the potential for hurt is minimised.

Section Five: Managing Your Own Development

Introduction

At the beginning of Section Two we wrote:

> 'Only if a trainer is actively engaged in their own development can they effectively contribute to the development of others.'

The trainer needs to have, readily accessible, personal experience of the complexity of learning, the struggle for the learner to take some control of the learning process. By engaging in their own personal and professional development, trainers gain first-hand understanding of the impact that the demands they make as trainers have on the people they train. Such experience and understanding enables them to develop relationships with other learners which are essentially equal, despite the difference in their position: both are people engaged in their own development.

Not only is the relationship more equal: the trainer can draw on their own experience of learning in order to help other learners. Awareness of their own tendency to set unrealistic targets, for example, helps them to understand and support people who are over- or under-ambitious. Awareness of their own blocks and resistances helps them to support people who are struggling to learn. Just as experience of the learners' profession will give a trainer credibility in the learners' eyes, so will experience of being a learner. And most importantly, awareness of your own limitations as a learner and developer will generate humility. It is this humility which mitigates the natural power of the position of 'teacher', which allows the learner 'in' on the learning process, and which gives them independence.

But we know how difficult it is for trainers to be 'actively engaged in their own development'! It's difficult to find the time, to make yourself and your development a priority, above all the other pressing needs and demands. It's difficult to find the sources of feedback and support that can be trusted and valued. And sometimes, it's difficult to listen to what they have got to say!

We wrote this book to provide a resource that trainers could use as a contribution to their own professional development. It is a tool with which to reflect on current practice and review options for the future. Section Five focuses more specifically on the process of managing your own development. In a sense, it is a microcosm of the book as a whole. We are inviting you to engage explicitly and actively in the processes that we have described as integral to our training methodology. Whereas before we were asking you to consider those processes in the light of your experience as a trainer, now we are asking you to apply those processes to yourself as a learner, so that you learn about how you manage your development at the moment, and can consider how you are going to manage it in the future.

To make this connection unavoidably clear, we have structured the section according to the five elements we described in Section Three: climate, support, stepping, challenge and reflection. We have provided an activity for each element which asks you to reflect on your current situation and identify, if appropriate, realistic steps that you could take to continue your development.

Climate

Organisations, like courses, have climates. Organisational climate is affected by internal and external influences. Groups of people working together develop unspoken ground-rules which govern how members of the group behave towards each other. The ground-rules generate an internal dynamic which often operates at an unconscious level: a ground-rule which says that it is OK to put colleagues down, for example, is usually not a conscious decision. A ground-rule which says never criticise a colleague in front of a client is probably a more deliberate attempt to control a working relationship.

External pressures also affect a group's working climate. Pressure of work, the level of resourcing, status within the organisation, the availability of recognition, the degree of expectation . . . these are all factors which influence a group's self-image and self-esteem. This in turn influences the climate within which the group works. And the climate will affect not just how members of the group interact with each other, but how they interact with their clients.

Two examples come to mind: first, a group of trainers from the training department of a large institution who unmistakably brought their climate with them onto a course. They were generally complacent and self-satisfied, not self-critical, and so unprepared for critical feedback. Second, a small group of trainers in local government who worked within a department which was bureaucratic and unsympathetic. The trainers felt that too much of their energy was spent in fighting the climate of their organisation.

Below is a table of 10 pairs of adjectives that could describe the climate of the group, organisation or situation that you work in. They are arranged as a series of opposites with a line connecting them. Place a cross on each line in the place which best describes the climate in which you work:

formal	....	informal
restricting	....	releasing
pressured	....	relaxed
unsupportive	....	supportive
unreflective	....	reflective
complacent	....	self-critical
unchallenging	....	challenging
self-indulgent	....	rigorous
insensitive	....	caring
blocking development	....	promoting development

You may have had a clear picture of the climate you work in before you did this exercise. On the other hand, you may not have thought about it in this way before. You may have been surprised by your own perceptions, or the strength of your feelings about one or more issues. People can become immune to their working conditions, believing them to be inevitable and unchangeable. In fact this is rarely true. Below is a set of questions to help you explore your relationship to your climate further:

1 *Are you satisfied with your working climate?* Does it give you the support and stimulation that you need for your professional development? Or does it hold you back, or divert your energy, or discourage you from taking the necessary risks?

2 *How do you contribute to your working climate?* Are you respon-

sible for providing the caring, for example? Do you challenge it by questioning people's attitudes and behaviour? Do you try to change it, by making demands of others, or offering your support? Or do you acquiesce, feeling that it's as good as it will get, or that you can't affect it, or that you can get by in spite of it?

3 *Are there things you want to change?* Is there a cross that you have placed too far along the left-hand side for comfort? For example, do you want to develop ways in which people can reflect on their work and get feedback from others? Is there one issue that has been bothering you for months that is colouring your whole attitude to your work, or your colleagues, or the organisation you work for?

Action plan

If there are areas of your working climate that you are strongly concerned about or dissatisfied with, you may want to take this opportunity to plan how you could change the situation. You may feel that this is unnecessary. Or you may feel that it is impractical, that there are too many factors preventing change. In our experience, there are always some steps that people can take which will improve things slightly. Seeing the situation as immutable is generally a form of resistance to change.

For example, you might feel that your organisation is complacent, that it always has been and always will be, and that there is nothing you can do. In order to get anywhere, you may need to redefine the problem: to personalise it. It may be more useful to see the problem as the fact that you don't get the critical feedback that you need. If other people in the organisation suffer from complacency, that is their responsibility. You can only take responsibility for yourself. There may be steps that you can take to get critical feedback which would be impractical at an organisational level. You could:

- ask a colleague to give you an appraisal of your work, inviting them to sit in on one of your courses if necessary;
- seek feedback from outside the organisation, from people that you train, for example, or from trainers from other organisations;
- ask for a formal appraisal interview, and suggest ways in which you would like the interview to be conducted.

Steps like these, which initially only benefit yourself, will also affect the climate as a whole. It may not change things as radically or as quickly as you would like. But believing that there should be a 'total' and 'instant' solution is another resistance strategy, a recipe for inertia!

If you do want to plan steps to change your climate, we suggest that you:

- initially focus on one issue or problem only;
- select an area which is not too far down the left-hand side of one of the lines: better to succeed with a small problem than fail with a big one;
- plan action that is realistic and that can be done soon;
- clearly identify your first step, and give yourself a deadline for carrying it out.

Support

Training can be a lonely business. It involves a large degree of giving: giving energy, support, encouragement, feedback. It involves working with people whom you may see only occasionally, sometimes only once, for the duration of a course or training event. We are frequently in the position, at the end of a course, of feeling drained and exhausted as we watch people leave with renewed energy and enthusiasm for their work. At times like these, we crave some support, some appreciation or acknowledgement of what we have given. And we know that it is inappropriate to ask for it at that moment.

Other trainers that we have talked to share these feelings. They too feel that they lack support, or that there is a disproportionate balance between what they give out and what they get back. From these discussions we realised two things: first that support can mean different things to different people; and second that people do have sources of support, but they tend not to make very good use of them.

Hank recently worked with a group who complained forcefully of feeling unsupported in their work. He asked them to be more specific: to say precisely what it was that they wanted. They generated a list which covered a number of areas: understanding of the complexity and demanding nature of their work; recognition of their skills and commitment; appreciation of the quality and care that they invested in their work; and, in a basic way, approval.

Having clarified what was meant by support, the group then identified the different sources of support that were available to them. They generated another list, which surprised them by its length. They had been focusing their feelings on the people who managed them, and in so doing had neglected to use other potential sources of support. In fact, their management team weren't in a position, for various reasons, to give them the support they wanted. The group had got trapped in a dynamic of expecting support from an inappropriate source. They ended up feeling frustrated and resentful, and not only unsupported but criticised by their management.

The group planned ways in which they could get the support they needed from other sources. This was obviously good for them, but it also had the effect of relieving pressure on their management. They stopped seeing the management as a source of support and so felt less resentful when that support wasn't forthcoming. In fact they were able to see that their two managers were probably in need of the same kinds of support that they had identified earlier: understanding, recognition, appreciation and approval.

Opposite is an example of a diagram which you can use to map out your support network. In the centre of the diagram is you. Radiating from that centre are two segments, each describing a possible area of support: one describes sources within your personal life; the other, sources within your professional network.

Draw lines outwards from the centre towards people who do or could give you support. The length of each line should illustrate the degree of support that you get at the moment: the shorter the line the greater the degree of support. On each line place arrows which indicate the direction in which the support flows: to you, from you, or both. Figure 2 shows how Jill used the diagram to map out her current support network.

Doing this exercise may have reaffirmed for you the degree of support that you get. On the other hand it may have left you feeling depressed about how unsupported you really are. To a large extent this will depend on your situation. Jill worked within a team who made a policy decision to make the time to meet together in order to support each other. For five years Hank worked on his own, continually feeling exposed and under-supported. You may work in a situation similar to these, or be somewhere in between: working in a team that snatches time for support as and when it can, for example.

Lack of support can be dangerous. If people feel undervalued, this tends to lead to an erosion of goodwill, a lowering of commitment and generosity. If people feel over-exposed, this tends to lead to burn-out, pendulum swings of emotion and a lowering of the ability to evaluate clearly. If people work in a vacuum, this tends to reduce confidence

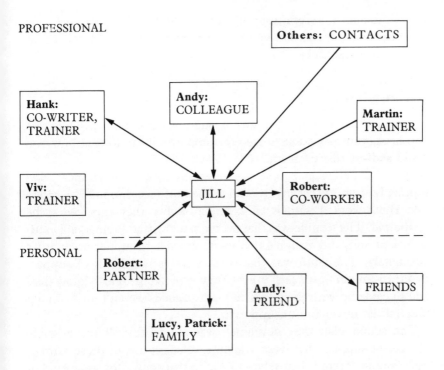

PROFESSIONAL

Figure 2: Jill's support network

and make development difficult. Below is a set of questions to help you review the degree and quality of the support you give and receive:

- *Are you satisfied with the degree of support you get at the moment?* Do you get enough support? Do you get too much, having to spend time in meetings which you think are unnecessary? Do you make full use of your support network, or do you focus your need for support on only a few people? Do you get support when you need it, or does it come to you in random, unplanned moments?
- *Are you satisfied with the quality of the support that you get?* Do you get the kind of support that you need — for example, do you get a lot of approval for your work when what you really want is feedback? Do you get support from people whose opinion you respect and value?
- *Are you satisfied with the support that you give?* Do you consider the needs for support of the people you work with? Do you offer unsolicited support to colleagues? Are you

generous in recognising and affirming the skills and achieve-
ments of others? Do you feel comfortable in giving colleagues
critical feedback?

Action plan

If you feel that you don't receive enough of the kind of support that
you need, you may want to take this opportunity to look at how you
could address this problem.

In our experience, people are reluctant to ask for support, and
especially support that involves an element of recognition. The group
that Hank worked with is an example of this: they expected to be
supported. The trouble was that people saw them as a remarkably self-
sufficient unit, and assumed that they were able to support each other
adequately. The truth was that there were certain kinds of support
that they couldn't give each other. They expected people to know that,
and to come up with the goods. When the goods weren't forthcoming
they felt let down and unsupported.

The action plan they developed was to identify all the possible
sources of support that were available, to select one of those sources
each, and to commit themselves to asking that source for some kind of
support. They planned to explain to people that they were coming to
them because they were feeling in need of support, and then ask them
for some specific pieces of feedback. In this way they were taking
responsibility for the problem — though none of them relished the
prospect at the time!

If you work closely with others, you may want to look at ways that
you could organise your working relationship to ensure that support is
available when needed. If you co-train with one or more other people
for example, a first step may be to ask for a discussion about ways in
which you could be more supportive of each other. Or you may need
to look at how you use the time you do make available for feedback so
that it is used to maximum advantage.

You may feel that you want to affect the general climate of your
work situation in order to make it more instinctively supportive. The
most effective way of doing this might be to model the degree and
quality of support you think is required by giving it to others, or by
asking one or more of your colleagues whether they too feel unsupported.

As a general rule, if you want support, you have to ask for it! And
the more specific you can make your request, the more likely it is to be

met. Support is an umbrella word that covers a range of more precise needs. Check out what it is that you want. And try to make sure that you ask people who are in a position to give it to you!

Stepping

As we said in the introduction to this book, most trainers have become trainers by accident rather than design. Few of the trainers that we know have received much training in being trainers. The odd short course here or there seems to be the norm. The bulk of a trainer's professional learning and development comes from experience. This places considerable emphasis on the need for conscious and planned self-management: the trainer has almost total responsibility for managing their own development.

Because development is based on experience, the nature of development will depend on the range and quality of the experiences available to the trainer. Running the same courses in the same way, working alongside the same people having the same expectations of you will tend to produce a high level of expertise and competency in one training approach or style. Working in a number of different contexts, alongside people with different experiences and expectations, will tend to produce a wide repertoire of styles and approaches with the risk of not fully exploring or developing expertise in any of them. Jill's development has generally followed the former scenario, whereas Hank's has been more along the lines of the latter.

In both instances, however, we were able to recognise the steps that we had taken, often unconsciously, to get us to where we are now. Those steps have taken a number of different forms. Some of them have been meeting with people who have provided a seminal influence on our work: Jill working with Leslie Button, for example, and learning about groupwork philosophy and technique; Hank meeting Jill and discovering active learning techniques through involvement with the Active Tutorial Work project that she co-directed with Andy Smith. Other steps have come from insights and realisations gained while running our own courses: certain courses stand out for both of us as times when we have taken a leap forward in terms of our understanding of learning processes and training technique. A third step has been provided by courses we have attended as learners: a profound influence on Hank's work has been learning about Contribution Training from courses run by the Pellin Institute in London.

In most of the above cases, none of those steps were planned. They happened, to a large degree, by accident, in the same way that we both became trainers by accident. The potential of each step to contribute to our development has been dependent on us having the time and commitment to reflect on new experience, and on us being able to integrate new learning with what we already know.

Opposite is an example of a diagram which you can use to review your development to date, and to plan steps that you could take to manage your future development. In the centre of the diagram is you. Above you and feeding into you are the seminal experiences that have contributed to your current stage of development. Figure 3 shows how Hank used the diagram to review his past development.

Filling in the diagram was very reaffirming, not to say reassuring! It helped us make sense of what has often felt like a disparate and incongruous history. And it made us think hard about how we used those steps, and particularly about whether we made enough use of them. If you have filled in your own diagram, you may have had similar responses. You may have already been well aware of the developmental steps that you have taken. You may have felt concerned that there weren't enough steps, or that there wasn't enough variety in them. You may have felt concerned, like Hank, about the random way in which the steps were taken, and about how little control you had over them.

The second part of the exercise is an opportunity to take a more controlled approach to your future development. This time, rather than looking at the steps that have led to where you are now, the exercise involves identifying the steps that you need to take in order to get to where you want to be in the future. Figure 4 shows the steps that Hank plans to take: some are steps that can be taken immediately — these are on the left hand side of the diagram, starting with the most immediate. Others are steps to be taken some time in the future — ending on the right hand side of the diagram with the step most distant from now.

Hank's steps involved a number of options:

- Co-training with colleagues that he doesn't normally run courses with is a step that is possible in the short-term, although not easy to organise.
- Becoming fully confident and competent in one set of materials before moving on to the next one is a real problem at the moment, given the current work situation; it requires a greater

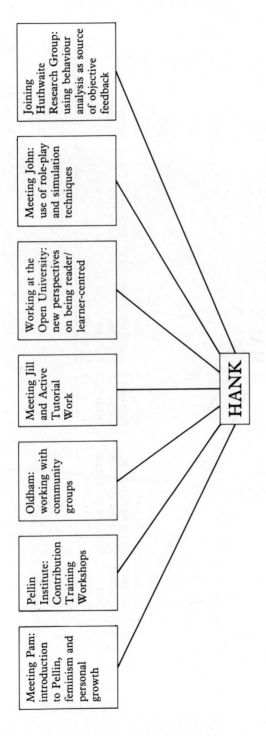

Figure 3: Hank: past development

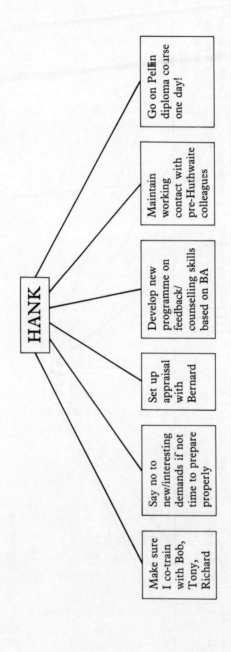

Figure 4: Hank: future development

degree of ruthlessness in saying 'no', especially to opportunities for new work that are interesting and exciting.

- Structuring feedback with people that he co-trains with at the moment is an immediate and achievable step.
- Working with new material, and particularly developing new material, is a step that will be necessary within the next six months anyway — the danger is in not allowing enough time for the development to be done properly.
- Working with trainers from outside Huthwaite is possible, but will require careful negotiation and planning.
- Going on courses for his own development is a bit of a pipe-dream; further training with the Pellin Institute is something that has already been put off twice, and will require Herculean efforts if it is ever to happen.

Hank saw his development in terms of consolidation of the existing alongside a continuing but more controlled exposure to the new and the different. You may have planned similar steps. If you identified a large number of disparate steps in the first part of the exercise, you may have been more concerned with consolidating and building on those experiences rather than in seeking out new ones. If your experience to date has stemmed from a narrow base of experience, you may want to seek opportunities to explore new approaches, witness different styles and techniques, or to experiment with new material.

Whatever the steps you have identified, the difficult bit is making sure that they happen! To make it easier, break each of the major steps you have identified through the diagram into the series of actions (or small steps) that you will need to take in order to ensure that the major step is achieved. Then focus your energy on achieving the first of the small steps. This may be simply to tell somebody about it, and ask them to support you to achieve it in some way.

It is worth bearing in mind the guidelines for action planning that we gave at the end of the discussion on climate earlier in this section:

- initially focus on no more than two of the steps that you have identified: perhaps the two nearest the left hand side, or one short-term step and one that is longer-term but which will need action to be taken now;
- make sure that at least one of the steps is achievable: better to succeed with a small step than fail with a big one;
- plan action that is realistic and that can be done soon;
- clearly identify your first step, and give yourself a deadline for carrying it out.

Challenge

In the training context, challenge refers to a planned activity or impromptu situation in which the learner is confronted by the risk of having to move beyond the familiar. The response to the challenge provides insight: learning at the self-awareness end of the developmental continuum. Challenge provides the most intense and profound learning experiences: people learn at a number of levels, but they especially learn about aspects of themselves with which they are not familiar.

This is also true in real life. Challenge is an essential ingredient of development. Professionally it can lead to the acquisition and development of new skills and repertoires, new insights and understandings, revised attitudes and relationships. Personally it can lead to greater self-awareness and self-control, and greater awareness of others and one's effect on others. Challenge provides stimulation, which in turn ensures sustained motivation and energy. It works against cosiness and complacency, and it demands creativity and flexibility.

Having said all that, challenge is difficult to specify. For some people, certain interpersonal actions are enormously challenging: making demands; giving negative feedback; showing or receiving affection, for example. For others, pragmatic actions can be a source of challenge: making decisions; carrying out unwanted tasks; finishing off tasks that are personally significant; persevering with the mundane. For some people the greatest challenge may be to allow themselves to relax, for others it may be to allow themselves to care. People tend to know what they find challenging, what they find difficult, the things they keep putting off. They also often know what they need to do to face that challenge. The trouble is doing it!

As trainers, we have often felt that there has been too much challenge in our lives. The act of standing up at the beginning of a course and winning over yet another group of unknown people is a continual challenge that we have to rise to. Giving and receiving feedback, both to course participants and to fellow trainers, is challenging. Learning or developing new material and finding ways of presenting it to learners is challenging, and so on. But as we become familiar with these features of our lives, their challenge loses its potency. This is not to say that they aren't challenging or risky: the adrenalin still flows, but we tend to know now that we will be all right. The challenge has less potency to contribute to our development.

We have both, in different ways, striven to seek out new challenges to ensure that we continually develop, to prevent us from hardening over, or from becoming stale, cynical or burnt out. 'Seek out' sounds a bit too deliberate. We have constantly been confronted with challenges, a number of which we decided to face: running training courses for senior managers; public speaking in front of large audiences; working in sensitive areas, such as the prevention of child abuse; working with new material; giving negative feedback to co-trainers. Looking back we can see that we developed strategies for dealing with these challenges, and drew on people for support whilst we dealt with them. So the following activity asks you to look back over some challenges you have faced in a similar way.

Draw up three columns with the following headings:

Challenges   Strategy used   Support received

Look back over the last year of your life and identify any challenges that you feel that you have faced during that time. These challenges may be either from your professional or personal life. It may have been to change job, for example, or it may have been to tell somebody how you feel about them. Now select the three challenges that you feel were the most significant, and place them in the left-hand column of the diagram below. Then fill in the rest of the diagram if you can, describing the way in which you faced the challenge, and the support, if any, that you received when you did so.

Some people will have been able to select three challenges easily. Others may have had more difficulty, either because there were too many to choose from, or because there were too few. It may be worth reflecting, at this stage, on the level of challenge that you feel comfortable with at this stage in your life and career. You may have been through a turbulent passage, for example, and are now craving a period of stability. On the other hand, you may be in a period of stability which you no longer feel comfortable with. You may work in a job that doesn't stimulate you any more, or you may have been avoiding risks because you don't feel confident of your own ability, or of the support of your peers. The following questions may help you to reflect on your current relationship to challenge:

- *Do you feel sufficiently challenged and stimulated in your work at the moment?*
- *Is your work itself challenging, or do you have to create your own challenges?*

• *Do you take on the challenges that present themselves to you through your work?*
• *Do you actively seek out situations or people that you think will provide you with challenge?*

Action plan

The next stage of the activity will be more relevant for you if you feel underchallenged at the moment. If you feel over-stretched, however, it may be useful to you as a way of prioritising the challenges which are most important to you, which will most nourish you, and from which you will get the greatest feelings of accomplishment. The diagram is the same as in the previous activity, but this time it is directed to the future. Select three challenges that you need to take in the next three months. These may be challenges that you have already identified through previous activities in this section: for example, your greatest challenge may be to take the first step in your future development; or it may be to seek support from a colleague. When you have selected your three challenges, describe the strategy required for you to meet those challenges, and identify the sources of support that you will need.

Future challenges   Strategy required   Support needed

Planning for future challenge, and especially prioritising challenges that will be nourishing and personally significant, is an important factor in managing your own development. We know how easy it is to be purely reactive, responding to challenging demands and getting caught up in a momentum over which we have little control. It is not generally possible to stop that momentum. But it is possible to ensure that at least some of the challenges it presents to you are ones of your own choosing, and ones which will give you the feelings of accomplishment needed to sustain your motivation and energy.

Whether the challenge is freely-chosen or imposed on you, it will contribute more to your development if you take conscious steps to plan how you are going to face it, and explore the support that you may need to help you. Support may take the form of telling someone that you are going to do something as a way of committing yourself to doing it. Or it may involve asking someone to take on the challenge with you. At the least, it should involve having someone who can help you to reflect on the nature of the challenge and your response to it after your response has been made.

Reflection

The activities in the previous parts of this section have been asking you to reflect backwards over your professional development to date, and to reflect forwards over the development that you would like to take place in the future. This has required you to stand back from your experience, to view it as objectively as possible, and to review your thoughts and feelings about what you see. We have provided you with a series of structures to give your reflection shape and purpose, but we weren't there, as we would be on a course, to clarify misunderstanding, to support your reflection, and to push you on to deeper levels of reflection. You will have made a series of choices, ranging from deciding whether to do the activities at all to selecting the level of intensity which you applied to them.

In this part of the section, we want to explore how you normally reflect on your experience: the conscious and unconscious steps that you take to process what happens to you, to interpret its meaning, and learn from it for the future. Our experience of being trainers is that there is a lot to process, and precious little time in which to do it. When we come off a course there is a mass of information swilling around in our heads: what the participants were like and how they responded; how we performed as trainers and as people; the structure and the material of the course itself; plus a whole series of random thoughts and ideas that occurred to us, only some of which were triggered by the preceding events. If the course has been difficult there will be a range of feelings, often uncomfortable feelings, that we will need to resolve in some way. There are events in the office, exchanges with colleagues, meetings, issues that we need to consider. And then there are events in our non-work lives, and the continual, difficult balancing act between our professional and personal needs. There is never enough time! Often the only time available is in the car, as we drive from one source of stimulation to the next.

We also know that if we don't make sufficient time for reflection, we pay the price, maybe not immediately, but eventually. Reflection is not just a process of making sense of experience, it is also a process of recovery and regeneration. If we don't take the time to recover from stressful situations, and to resolve our feelings about those situations, we will carry them into the next event, and will therefore be less able to respond to that event on its merits. The feelings we carry with us will colour our responses and affect our ability to evaluate clearly and retain a sense of perspective. If we don't make the time to recharge our batteries, we get tired, our intuition and sensitivity become blunted, we get burnt out. And this gets communicated, inevitably, to the people we are working with.

The personal agenda is set alongside the need to review our work as an essential element of developing the effectiveness of our approaches and material, and also our effectiveness as trainers. We find that it is easier to make time for this kind of reflection, partly because it is easier to justify spending time on it, and partly because it usually involves getting feedback or advice from others, whether they are colleagues or course participants. Nevertheless, we still don't spend as much time as we would like on reviewing our work, and we have to structure the time we do take as much as possible to ensure that the maximum benefit is derived from it. Without structure, it is difficult to cover all the issues, and to make sure that the most important issues are covered in the time available. The structure may also need to determine the method of discussion: it may be appropriate for one person to clear their head of thoughts and then get feedback; it may be more useful for another person to act as questioner, controlling the discussion with strategic questions to uncover the real issues; each person may need to have a clear opportunity to speak, and give their uninterrupted thoughts. Structure controls both content and process.

The options for reflection can be broadly defined as follows:

alone structured	alone unstructured
with others structured	with others unstructured

Use this diagram now in two ways to review how you reflect:

1 List the kinds of issues that you reflect on in each box. For example, you may find that you don't reflect on anything alone in a structured way, but that you reflect on personal issues alone unstructured. You may reflect on a course with your co-trainer in a structured way, and have general discussions about work with colleagues in an unstructured way. Try to be as specific as possible about the kinds of issues you reflect on in each of the different boxes.

2 Review your 'reflection budget'. Like us, you probably have a limited amount of time for reflection. Look on the total time you have available as a budget, and use the diagram to explore how you spend your budget. For example, if you only ever have the opportunity to reflect alone in an unstructured way, you will be spending 100% of your budget in that way. If you have regular team meetings to discuss issues, this may represent 20%, say, of your total budget.

You may have found this activity difficult: it is not always easy to distinguish between 'solo' structured and unstructured reflection, for example. And it can be hard to separate personal and work-related issues, the boundary between them is often invisible (which is not to say that it doesn't exist). Like all the activities in this section, you may also have found it reaffirming or depressing depending on your situation. Your organisation may take reflection seriously, and provide adequate time and structures for that purpose. At the other extreme, you may work on your own most of the time, and have no recourse for reflection with others. The following questions may help you to clarify your needs before thinking about steps you could take to modify the amount and quality of your reflection:

- *Are you satisfied with the amount of time you make available for reflection?*
  Is it enough for you to keep up-to-date with your thinking and feeling responses to events in your life?
- *Are you satisfied with the way you use the time you do make available?*
  Is there sufficient structure to your reflection? Do you use other people enough to get feedback or advice?
- *If you do structure your reflection, either alone or with others, are you satisfied with the structures that you use?*
  Does your structure allow for prioritisation of issues, for example?
  Does it enable you to explore issues in sufficient depth?

You may have noticed that we have talked about *making* time available, rather than *having* time available. When we have worked with people on reflection, the most common complaint is that there just isn't the time. Our response is to ask people to take responsibility for this, to say: 'I don't make the time'. Although they readily admit the importance of reflection, people rarely give it sufficient priority to make sure that it happens. This is true for us as trainers: we have to struggle to safeguard time for reflection on courses. The time is there — it's up to us to decide how to use it. For most people, whatever they say, reflection tends to be a low priority. This is partly because it is difficult to do well, and partly because it can often be demanding and uncomfortable.

All of which means that when time for reflection is made available, it has to be time well spent. People need to come away feeling that they have achieved something, something more than an interesting conversation or set of thoughts. If the time given over to reflection is perceived to be beneficial in concrete ways, people are more likely to make more time available. Identifying the outcomes for any period of reflection can help to create a clear sense of purpose, as well as providing a checklist with which to review the effectiveness of the reflection process. Agreed outcomes can lead naturally to a structure for achieving those outcomes which provides shape and direction. However effective your reflection is, it's still likely that effort will be needed to make time available, or to persuade others to make time available. Having clear in your own mind what the pay-offs are for you in making that effort will help you to make it.

Action plan

If your answer to one or more of the questions above has been 'No, I am not satisfied', you may want to take this opportunity to plan ways in which you could improve the quantity and quality of the time you have for reflection.

1 Decide which kind of reflection you want to work on. You may want to create more time in which you can reflect on your own in an unstructured way. Or you may want to take steps to institutionalise a more formal reflection process with your colleagues at work. You may feel that you need both. Rather than tackling everything at once, however, prioritise the kind of reflection that you feel you would most benefit from at the moment, and which you can achieve most easily.

2 Identify the steps you need to take in order to improve the situation. This may involve planning how to safeguard time against interruption. For example, you could claim a half-hour to yourself when you get home from work when you can think back over what has happened during the day. Or you could organise a weekly co-counselling session with a friend or colleague when

you can debrief each other over the events of the preceding week and plan strategies for the week ahead. Or you could agree with your co-trainer to have a regular feedback session at the end of every course.

3 Plan how you are going to take this step. It may involve 'selling' the idea to colleagues: how could you present your proposal most persuasively? It may involve selling the idea to yourself: how can you make sure that you will take the steps that you have identified? It may help to identify a fall-back position, a compromise which means that, if you find that you can't achieve your ideal, at least you will have achieved some improvement.

4 Identify what outcomes you want from your reflection. There are a range of possible outcomes. You may want, for example, to get specific feedback about your performance as a trainer; to give feedback to others; to review training processes and materials; to explore alternative approaches; to express accumulated feelings; to get advice about current problems or difficulties.

5 Plan how your time could be structured so that your outcomes can be achieved. In our experience, reflection is helped by questioning. This can occur naturally within free-ranging discussion, but is usually best managed if questions are pre-planned, or if somebody takes responsibility for formulating and asking questions. As in courses, the level of reflection may need to be stepped, allowing for increasing personalisation and intensity. This should be borne in mind within each period for reflection and also as part of your long-term strategy. If you can make regular time available, you could plan to consciously develop your reflective skills as one of the desired outcomes of the reflection process.

Summary

There is a danger that we will have come across in this section as paragons of self-development. This is far from the truth! We have learnt much from our struggles to maintain some control over how we develop professionally, but we still find it hard to put that learning into practice. When we did the activities that we wrote for this section, we found them difficult, revealing, often painful. We realised how little time we gave over to looking after ourselves, to identifying and meeting our own needs. The activities enabled us to firm up some of the vague promises that we had made to ourselves, and to plan ways in which they could be transformed from wishful thinking to reality. We hope they have done the same for you.

This section has also provided a different perspective on the possible applications of the five elements. We use them in a number of ways. Most often we use them as a guide for planning training courses and events. Hank also uses them as an 'audit' for work-teams, taking them through each element as a way of reviewing their current way of working together, and as a tool for planning change. Jill uses them increasingly when she is training trainers. In the next section we describe how they can be used up-front on a training course, so that participants are learning about the use of the elements and experiencing their application at the same time. You may find it useful, at this stage, to consider whether there are any ways in which you could apply the elements within your own work context before you move on to Section Six.

Section Six: The Elements In Action

Introduction

Since finishing the other sections of the book, Jill has run a course on Active Learning in Education for a local education authority, in which she overtly applied the five elements described in Section Three as the basis for the programme. Section Six is a description of what happened on this course. It gives you a perspective on the five elements in action, and also provides you with details of some of the activities we use. Although the course was dealing specifically with issues in secondary education, we hope that you will be able to extract from this account ways of relating the issues we have been discussing in this book to the contexts in which you work. And we hope to communicate some of the vitality and excitement which the occasion generated.

The background

The course was organised by the LEA to support a project working on Records of Achievement in secondary schools. The participants were head teachers, college principals, deputies and advisers. This group had been meeting together, and experimenting in their own institutions, for three years. A policy paper stated that: '. . . students should be encouraged to become increasingly involved in their own learning and self-assessment' and that '. . . the process of learning would be the vehicle for helping students to become so involved'. There had been some attempt to make the in-service and business meetings of the project group more informal and participatory. Although the members of the group knew each other quite well, very well in some cases, it was felt by the advisers that there was now a need

to tackle the group's understanding of the learning process for themselves.

There would be thirty people altogether, including two observers.
The observers' role was to record the event for the purpose of the
overall monitoring and evaluation of the project. There was always at
least one observer at each meeting or in-service session, but it was
rarely the same people who filled this function. The observers and
their role were to play a significant part in the events of the course. Jill
spent some time discussing with the adviser organising the course
what the precise objectives were, and who those objectives had come
from. Her brief was to 'involve them in active learning, so that they
will understand for themselves that the processes of learning are
equally as important as the content'. The course organiser had also
told her that people would be reluctant to get involved, and that they
had specifically asked that the theories about active learning be
'expounded' by 'these experts'. They were not prepared to 'simply
learn from experience'!

This is a familiar dilemma to trainers: whose problem is it? Was the
adviser accurately reporting the mood of the learners? Or was she
revealing her own anxieties? Would the best approach be to concede to
the expressed wishes and start with theoretical input, before gently
moving the learners towards a more participatory role? Or would it be
better to involve them in revealing their resistance right at the start?
Jill and her co-trainer, when planning the programme, decided to play
safe. Her instinct, based on previous experience of this kind of group,
prompted a feeling that a 'straight in at the deep-end' strategy was too
great a risk. She also trusted the adviser's judgement.

It was a two-day course, but guest speakers had already been arranged
for the first day. Jill decided to go to the first day anyway, in order to
'read' the atmosphere and get to know people informally. This would
be the first step in establishing a relationship between herself and her
co-trainer and the learners. Having told the course organiser that she
would be coming early, it was suggested that she could have the last
session on the first day. This presented Jill with the problem of what
to do in that session. She had already decided to start the second day
with a straight input to introduce the essential elements of active
learning before moving into practical application. But the first two
sessions on the first day were also going to be straight lectures. The
learners would be sitting passively for about three hours altogether.
Giving them yet another input, even though they had asked for it,
would be counter-productive. The 'brick walls' put up as a defence

against becoming involved would be so high they might be insurmountable.

This was the compromise solution: the input would be succinct and to the point; Jill would be disciplined in the delivery and not get carried away; there would be short breaks when the learners would be asked to address a specific question about the content of her input so far; they would be asked to do this with two or three people sitting near; they would be given a set of hand-outs which would be incomplete and would require them to make their own notes to amplify things as the session went along.

As things turned out, the first speaker was unable to come after all. The organisers were worried as to how to fill the gap. Jill was more than happy to solve the problem by taking over the extra time. This provided the space to extend the initial input and deliver a more leisurely introduction.

The programme

Session 1

Using an overhead projector, Jill introduced the five elements which we consider to be the essential ingredients in the process of effective learning. She called up a great deal of energy to paint word pictures of real scenarios, using several examples from her own experience of working in classrooms to make the input stimulating and relevant. It felt a bit like a performance but she felt that this was what was needed to set the scene for what was to come.

She gave the learners a hand-out for each of the five elements, and asked them to add their own notes while she spoke. These notes would be referred to during the next day when they would experience for themselves the elements in action. The hand-outs contained the following information:

Handout 1:

CLIMATE

Provides reassurance

Releases energy

Engenders support

Generates motivation and commitment

Prepares for challenge

Establishes needs and goals

Shifts focus from teaching to learning

TEACHER'S ROLE

Recognising existing climate

Gaining support of opinion leaders

Sharing ownership of learning process

Consolidating commitment

Handout 2:

SUPPORT

Promotes a sense of belonging

Enhances self-esteem

Encourages motivation to keep trying

Is the forerunner to facing challenge

Is a key factor in learning how to learn

Develops skill in reflection

TEACHER'S ROLE

Shifting the focus towards the learners supporting each
other

Enabling support to be made available between the
learners

Ensuring that the support is effective

Being aware of the quality of relationships in the
learner group

Handout 3:

STEPPING

Maintains pace in learning

Develops depth

Builds up skills incrementally

Promotes a sense of achievement

Encourages motivation

Is a bridge between support and challenge

TEACHER'S ROLE

To be aware of:

warming up

group forming

group working

application

reviewing

Handout 4:

CHALLENGE

Stretches the learner

Exposes the learner

Promotes new learning

Builds confidence

Develops support and sensitivity

Encourages the taking of responsibility

TEACHER'S ROLE

Recognising readiness

'Stepping' new challenge

Engendering support

Holding back

Structuring reflection

Handout 5:

REFLECTION

Interprets experience

Turns experience into learning

Promotes new action

Develops reviewing skills

Encourages responsibility for learning

TEACHER'S ROLE

Planning time for reflection

Devising ways to develop reviewing skills

Helping to draw out support to aid reflection

Clarifying that reflection is a significant learning experience

After some small group discussion about the questions that each of the participants had identified, the session was over. There had been a lot of information-giving by Jill, but the group had been riveted by what she was saying. She felt she had paced the session well and had started to create a positive climate. The room they were in was too small to allow for much movement though. It was too hot and airless. And they had been in it too long. Jill asked for a different room for the rest of the course.

Session 2

The decision to change rooms was a big step in creating the climate for learning. The new room was bigger, cooler, with smaller but still comfortable chairs which were easy to move. The change helped the learners to accept a more active role. Plus they were 'heartily sick of sitting and being talked at' as one person remarked.

There are many and various activities from which to choose to create climate. Jill decided to start with 'Find someone who . . .'. Armed with pieces of paper printed with a variety of category statements, the participants were asked to put the names of other participants beside relevant statements. The categories had been chosen to suit a group who claimed to know each other quite well, and also to generate a light atmosphere. For example:

Find someone who:
* got up late this morning
* owns an E registered car
* knows the capital of Morocco

This caused much laughter and release of tension. It was followed quickly by forming pairs with the task of getting everyone's first name down on the piece of paper provided (one piece per pair). It revealed that most people did not, in fact, know everyone's name.

Jill then asked the pairs to sit down in their own space in the room (ie not too near another pair) and consider the climate which had been engendered and compare it with the climate during the first session. She and her co-trainer had to work hard to persuade the pairs to move their chairs away from the edges of the room and use up all the available space. She drew attention to the fact that this is part of the facilitator's role in managing the learning environment. She would continue to draw their attention to what she and her co-trainer were doing to nurture the climate during the course. These pointers were to help the learners to see the underlying processes at work, and to understand that climate can be managed and shouldn't just be left to chance.

The co-trainer led an activity which involved the pairs in thinking about what makes for effective learning. The change of voice was useful since they had been listening to Jill's voice for most of the afternoon. He asked them to individually remember a 'good' learning experience, 'good' because they knew that they had learned something; or they didn't learn much but it was enjoyable; or for whatever reason they might have for remembering it under the category of 'good'. It didn't necessarily have to be a school or childhood experience. The instructions were:

1 *Describe it to your partner. You have five minutes each.*
2 *Now, by yourself, write down key words and phrases which you have used whilst describing your experience.*
3 *Now do the same for a 'bad' learning experience. It may have been 'bad' because it was painful; or because you didn't learn anything; or for any other reason which makes you recall the occasion.*

The atmosphere in the room grew quiet as people began to work together. To signal the greater sensitivity required, the co-trainer had used a quieter tone to introduce the 'bad' learning experience, and had given an experience of his own as an example. This was a direct step in engendering support amongst the group.

Now the pairs moved into fours. They compared the key words and phrases and highlighted those which were common to all four of them. These were written up by Jill on a flip-chart while the co-trainer moved from group to group keeping the process as dynamic as possible. Individuals could also add to the corporate list any key word or phrase of their own about which they felt strongly but which had not been common to their group. One such contribution under the heading of 'bad' was 'anger, hate and revenge'!

Jill de-briefed the activity. She reminded the group that all the responses displayed came out of real experiences and asked:

What does this tell us about learning?

By now the learners were relaxed, willing to contribute, listening to one another, and engaged in the activity. Jill's next question was:

What about what we have just done as a learning experience?

Reflections about the climate, the way they had felt, things they had realised through being involved were expressed. Jill explained the process, which is called 'structured conversation', and pointed out that:

- everyone had been involved and everyone was able to make a contribution;
- the process can be used in many different contexts, only the content of the agenda for conversation needs to change;
- structured conversation is her most common way of establishing a conducive climate for learning.

The session finished with a final activity, one that was 'fun', but with two main underlying purposes: to end the day on an 'up-note'; and to leave some 'food for thought' about teaching and learning to carry over to the next day.

The activity was a history 'time-line'. The instructions were:

1 *Form a line across the room according to the date when you think that your house was built.*
2 *Form groups around the decade nearest to the date of your house. For example, if you thought it was built in 1935 you can join the 1930 or 1940 group.*
3 *Consider a range of questions chosen from the following examples:*

- What kind of family first lived in your house? (If yours is the first, describe your own family)
- What do you think the family's quality of life was/is like?
- What international, national, and local events might have affected/affect the family? How?
- What prospects would there be/are there for a fourteen year old teenager in that family?
- What are the prospects for a fourteen year old in the year 2050?

The group enjoyed helping one another with their historical memory. They liked talking about their houses, and remembering events where applicable. There was much debate about their projections into the future. Jill stopped them after a few minutes of discussion around each question, having suggested that a different person start each time. She took some reflection from one or two groups, taking care that every group could make a contribution throughout the activity. The contributions were informal, not made through a spokesperson. The whole group began to share an identity. The activity took half an hour. They could have gone on for hours. They had shared something of

themselves during this final session, and this was a step towards forming the working support groups for the major tasks she had planned
for the next day. It had been a long afternoon, but a good start!

Day 2: Session 3

Jill began the day by reminding the group:

- that they were experiencing at first hand the elements which she
  had described in her talk the previous afternoon;
- that they had hand-outs to refer to on which it would be useful
  for them to continue to make notes from their own experience of
  the elements as they unfolded;
- that this session was going to focus on support;
- that the session yesterday had focused on establishing a climate;
- that this morning they would start with more work on climate,
  as they would need to re-establish the climate that had been
  created the previous day.

To emphasise this last point, she asked how people were feeling right
now. Their responses confirmed the need for a 'warm-up' exercise,
followed by an activity which prepared for the work which was to
come. After all, it *was* Monday morning!

The 'warm-up' activity was 'Verbal tennis'. The instructions were:

1 *Form pairs and stand close together facing each other.*
2 *Do a word association exercise bound by certain categories which we
   will give you. For example, if the category was 'countries', it might go
   something like this: 'Chile' — 'Argentina' — 'Spain' — 'France' etc.*
   The categories were stepped from general areas like 'capital
   cities', increasing in relevance to the last category, which was
   'names of LEAs which are piloting Records of Achievement'.
3 *Swap partners between each category.* Jill explained that she
   wanted people to move about as a way of generating some physical energy for the day ahead.

Briefly, Jill pointed out what the activity had done for the climate in
the room, and described the ways in which it could be used in a classroom setting. She then introduced the next activity, called 'Information exchange'. She had chosen this because it would develop the
identity of the group, and would also demonstrate what she meant by
co-operative learning. The instructions were:

1 *On your own, think of all the sources from which you acquire knowledge.* eg travel, reading, the media, study of your subject, hobbies.

2 *Select a piece of general knowledge that other people in the room are unlikely to know.*

3 *Form a question, like a quiz question, based on this piece of knowledge. You must know the answer.*

4 *Write the question down (legibly but without giving your identity away) and fold up the piece of paper.*

5 *All stand up and pass the pieces of paper around the group. The object is to get rid of your own piece of paper and make sure you have someone else's, without knowing whose it is.*

6 *Find the answer to the question on your piece of paper. The answer is held by someone in the room.*

Often groups feel that this is too much like a party game, and this group were no exception. Some of them found it difficult to think of anything that they knew anything about. They covered up with jokes and laughter. The trainers had to gently help them to identify a question. During the exchange of papers the joking continued.

When people started searching for the answers to their questions a number of dynamics started to emerge. Some people refused to give answers, even to the question that they had written. Others had received approximate answers, not from the originator of the question. Some people had given up. Some people had received help from other people who had suggested possible leads to the one who might know. Others had received complete red-herrings!

When most people were finished, Jill stopped the activity, even though answers to several questions had not been found. Jill asked those still 'seeking' to read out their questions, and then for the originators to give their answers. One woman explained that she had found out her piece of information during an exotic holiday abroad. This provoked a lot of jocularity and sexist comments about her husband being able to afford to take her on expensive holidays. Jill picked up on this, asking the people responsible why they had done it. They blustered. Jill commented on whether this was an indicator of the quality of their relationships within the group.

Then somebody accused someone else of withholding their answer. Jill pointed out that a number of people had done the same. She asked them why, and whether this was another indicator of the quality of their relationships. Several agendas were beginning to emerge, and the pennies were beginning to drop. Jill deliberately brought their attention back to the activity, not wanting to get caught up in those issues too deeply at that point. The group began to see that the activity was more than a party game. It had involved them in:

- seeing familiar people in a new light;
- further exploring relationships within the group;
- uncovering issues that were getting in the way of the group working effectively together;
- understanding the issues involved in developing climate and support.

The session ended. Time for coffee.

Session 4

Jill explained that the objective for this session was to consolidate support and introduce challenge. She asked the course members to work in the small groups which they had formed the previous evening. The first exercise was to find things in common within each group. A few minutes later, once the level of energy in the room had risen, she introduced the first of the two main activities. This was an exercise in co-operative learning. The main features and stages of the process were as follows:

1 Reading individually a dense three-page text which was a glossary of terms used in Economics, and an explanation of their meaning. The reading represented a direct teaching input in a typical lesson. They were given five minutes to assimilate the text, so as to experience how a learner feels when they are being bombarded with information.

2 Completing statements lifted from the text in order to demonstrate understanding of terminology. Each person, in their small groups, attempted a statement in turn, and the others helped them until the whole group was satisfied by their explanation. Referring to the text was not allowed: they had to rely on their collective memory and existing knowledge.

3 Applying the knowledge acquired during the first two stages in a decision-making exercise. Case studies were provided concerning the siting of various industrial units, such as a factory for precision engineering. Each case study contained a variety of possible solutions. The groups had to agree on the best solution.

4 Reflecting on how they dealt with the activity as a group, as well as on what had been learnt about Economics.

When they had finished reflecting on the first activity, Jill led them straight into the second one. The same groups were presented with the task of solving a code which was presented on cards in the form of algebraic equations. Each person in the group had different cards, each one containing several 'clues', which represented the knowledge and expertise brought by each individual to the group. The key instructions were that:

1 *Everyone must keep hold of their own cards.* (This means that everyone has to take part. It helps them to feel that they have a contribution to make towards finding a solution, and prevents them from handing over responsibility to one or two members of the group.)
2 *Everyone must understand how each stage in arriving at the solution was reached.*

These two activities took one hour. When they were finished, Jill de-briefed the whole group, asking general questions such as, 'How have you felt during these two tasks?'. People commented on feeling supported, on enjoying working in groups, on how they had learnt things. Some people described how their initial reactions had been to withdraw from the activity — they hated maths, felt that they were inadequate, that they had nothing to contribute. But, as the activity progressed, they had become increasingly involved, and, because of encouragement from the group, they had been able to contribute towards reaching a solution.

The activities demonstrated to the group that, by placing emphasis on the process as well as the content of learning, climate and support can be established and developed in a relatively short time. People were visibly enjoying and benefiting from the supportive and companionable learning environment which had developed.

There was a short break. And then it was time to introduce 'Challenge'.

Session 5

Jill had given a great deal of thought to the kind of task which she thought this group would perceive as a challenge, given the short amount of time available and the fact that there were as many as thirty people on the course. She had decided that the best form of challenge would lie in handing over the responsibility for their learning to them. The task for the afternoon was to:

1 *Find two other people who share similar concerns around the issue of Records of Achievement. Agree, as a group of three, on how you can best spend the first hour of the afternoon to deal with those concerns. You may, for example, decide that the most useful way of spending the time is to tell each other about what steps you have taken within your own institutions.*

2 *Choose a 'resource person' from a pool made up of the members of the Core Team who have been responsible for steering and leading the project during the past three years. They should be the person who you think is best placed to help you with your task.*

Jill had worked out that there was one resource person per group, and had gone to some trouble to brief the Core Team about the nature of the activity. She had explained carefully to each one individually the purpose of the session: how it would be set up, and what their function would be. She had asked for, and gained, their agreement to act as resource people.

She suspected that people would want to form different groupings, working with friends and colleagues rather than people they were less familiar with. She also thought that they would want to work with particular members of the resource group. In fact, she was convinced that they would want to cluster together in large groups with two or three resource people tagging on. If she allowed them to do this, she would be letting them take the easy option, staying with what was comfortable, with what they already knew. They would be avoiding the challenge of seeking out new learning.

She outlined the task for the afternoon and itemised clearly what they needed to do now, before lunch, as preparation:

1 *Form your groups of three.*
2 *Decide how you want to spend the time available to you for this activity.*
3 *Make sure that each person feels that they will derive some benefit from this opportunity.*
4 *Choose your resource person and invite them to join you.*
5 *Decide where and when you will meet after lunch.*

She then sat back and waited. Several things happened, almost simultaneously.

A group of four friends converged on each other in the middle of the room, had a quick 'confab', and collared another friend who happened to be one of the resource people. They made for the door believing they had 'cracked' it — to be stopped by the co-trainer who had positioned himself there for this very reason. He pointed out that there were five in their group and that perhaps they shouldn't leave until all the groups were settled and all the negotiations had been completed. They stayed, still standing by the door.

At the same time the two observers, who had been joining in up to now, as well as making notes of the proceedings, said that they couldn't join a group of three as they wanted to be free to go in and out of all the groups. Jill said they should make this intention clear to the whole group, pointing out that it would upset the numbers. One of them stood up to do this by asking for people's attention. But at that precise moment one of the resource people said, in a loud voice:

'Just a minute! I feel very unhappy about this.'

She was closely followed by another resource person who said that he too was feeling threatened. There was a stunned silence. Jill had been expecting a certain amount of turbulence, but not quite so soon, and not from that particular quarter. She did three things:

1 She asked everyone to sit down, herself standing quite still and calm.
2 She itemised the issues which had arisen and which needed to be dealt with.
3 She supported the person who had expressed her feelings so forcibly by gently asking her to say more about how she felt.

The woman was still nervous and angry. She said she didn't like having to wait to be chosen: 'What if I'm *not* chosen?'. Everyone listened intently, looking at Jill to see how she was reacting, what she was going to do.

The woman had voiced what many in the room were feeling: they found the prospect of negotiating their own groups intimidating. She spoke again, saying directly to Jill: 'You set this up, it's your responsibility! You are destroying all the support which you have generated up to now'.

Jill did not respond immediately. She deliberately let silence reign, and waited for a response from within the group. Someone finally said: 'No! It is our responsibility to work this out, to take away the threat'.

Before Jill could build on this, however, someone else broke in quite heatedly with another objection: 'I'm not happy with this business of the observers'.

That then emerged as one of the real issues. For the whole three years of the project there had been observers at meetings. Their role and function had been explained but there had been no discussion, no opportunity for the group members to voice their feelings about it. Until now. A number of people spoke up: 'I've never been happy with observers: I don't like being watched'; 'I don't like to feel that what I say is being written down'. Someone proposed that now was not the time to resolve the issue, but that it must be on the agenda at their next business meeting. There was a general murmur of agreement.

Meanwhile the two observers, having conferred with each other, announced that they wanted to join in the activity this afternoon after all. 'We don't feel we can offer much to a group because our normal work is not directly related to this project. We are only here because we were asked to fill the role of observers for this course. But we want to know more about it'.

Again there was a general murmur of satisfaction at this.

The time was not right to take the group back to the original task of forming the working groups. Jill decided to help the group in making their decisions. She felt that the step of challenge which she had set up, handing over all the responsibility in one fell swoop, had been a 'step too far', and that she needed to make a bridging step which would ease them into it. It had exposed tensions and other 'agendas' which couldn't be fully resolved now. She needed to channel the group's energy into something positive, so that they could feel good about themselves again.

She made two proposals: first, that everyone should spend a little time identifying what their main concerns were, and then move around sharing these concerns with others. Perhaps then they would more easily be able to form their groups of three. Second, that the resource people should also meeet to identify what their particular individual skills, knowledge and experience were, so that they would be better able to match their individual expertise to the appropriate small group, rather than wait to be chosen.

Whilst her co-trainer facilitated the group forming, Jill worked with the resource group. They also needed to discuss what it meant to be a resource person. They had not considered themselves in that light before. They hadn't fully considered the implications when they had originally agreed to take on the role.

The whole group quickly gathered momentum. The groups formed naturally and easily. People were very much more aware of the needs of other people and took steps to make sure that everyone was included satisfactorily. They had been made aware of *climate* and *support* at an intellectual level. Now they were acting on this awareness and taking responsibility for these elements themselves.

The resource people started to move around the groups to find out where they could be most useful. Some of them still felt vulnerable, that they had nothing to offer, that no group would perceive them as a resource. But they began to support each other, deciding jointly who had the skills to match the different issues and concerns that had been identified.

Everything was now ready for the afternoon session. There was an air of purpose in the room. They had come through a period of turbulence and challenge together. The group was a different group.

Session 6

The groups met with their resource people. Jill and her co-trainer went for a short walk! They did not feel it appropriate to move round the groups in view of what had been said about observers. Also they did not want to take back any of the power which people were now exercising for themselves. When they came back, they observed from a distance how the groups were operating, especially how the resource people were fulfilling their role. Some of them appeared to have taken over and were doing most of the talking, lecturing in one case. There was still a lot to be learnt! But a good start had been made.

During the break for tea at the end of this session the discussions carried on. There was still energy, but the group was flagging. It felt like it had been a long day. Which meant that some more energy had to be generated for the final session.

Session 7

'Reflection should not be the "downer" at the end of the activity. It should be an intense activity in its own right'. We quote our own words from the chapter in Section Three on reflection. Words which we acknowledge are not easy to turn into actions.

Jill started this last session by asking everyone to move around and shake hands. She explained that this was an energiser to 'see us through' the last session, but also that it was a way of marking the working partnerships which had been formed. If she had asked them to do this at any other point in the course there would have been some embarrassed reactions. Now they could understand what it was for. One person put it succinctly: 'I can see now that you are in fact changing the focus to learning rather than it being on teaching'.

Before moving into reflection, Jill reminded them of the missing element: stepping. She hadn't planned a separate session around this element, as it didn't readily lend itself to that treatment. She referred directly to the turbulence of the session before lunch, explaining that she and her co-trainer were partly responsible for it because they had taken too big a step at the beginning. She used the proposals she had eventually made to facilitate the group-forming as examples of inserting steps into a process. And then she led a discussion about ensuring that the appropriate steps were taken in leading into challenging activities.

When the discussion on stepping was finished, she asked the group to find the person with whom they had had the structured conversation the previous evening. When they had formed their pairs, she asked them to help each other to review the whole course, and in particular the 'steps' they had taken to get to where they were now. She suggested that the hand-outs they had been given at the beginning would be a useful tool for this review. A starting point could be to refer back to the notes they had made on their hand-outs during her initial introduction. Perhaps they would be able to fill in some more of the gaps now.

The framework for this review was:

Remember: Help each other to remember the events and activities as they happened. Stick to facts, try not to stray into interpretations just yet.

Reflect: Which events or activities do you remember most? Why? How would you describe some of the emotions you have felt? How do they compare with those of your partner?

Review: Formulate two or three questions which you could ask of another pair to help them to recognise some learning which they have gained from this course.

This last step was a deliberate attempt to inject a new dynamic into the final session. People were tired and relaxed, but it was important that they take their reflection seriously. Asking them to work for other people forced them to take more responsibility for the reflection process, and to become more energetically involved. In planning how best they could help the other pair, they were also thinking about their own learning: 'What would help me to think about what I have learned? Could I answer that question? Is that too superficial?' etc.

The fours formed and the questions were asked. Once more there was an air of purpose in the room. Jill interrupted their animated conversations to introduce the last stage of the reflection process:

> *Resolve*:   Now think about the ways in which you will be able to use what you have learned on the course. What effects do you think it will have on what you do in the future? You may not be able to identify anything specific just at this moment, but if anything occurs to you now, or has occurred to you earlier on the course, share it with each other.

There was more animated conversation, which again Jill had to interrupt. She went round each of the fours, asking them what future action, if any, they had been able to identify. A number of significant points came out, particularly to do with how the group wanted to work together in the future.

The course was over. The trainers thanked everybody for their hard work and commitment. The course organiser, on behalf of the group, thanked the trainers.

Reading list

Reflection: Turning Experience into Learning
Edited by David Boud, Rosemary Keogh, David Walker.
Kogan Page, 1985   ISBN   0 85038 864 3

Experiential Learning: Experience as the Source of Learning and Development
David A Kolb
Prentice Hall, 1984   ISBN   0 13 295261 0

Impro
Keith Johnstone
Methuen, 1981   ISBN   0 413 46430 X

Choices
David Settle and Charles Wise
Basil Blackwell, 1986   ISBN   0 631 90129 9

Discovery and Experience
Leslie Button
Hodder and Stoughton

Awakening the Inner Eye: Intuition in Education
Noddings and Shore
Teachers' College, Columbia University, 1984

Learning in Action
Roger Kirk
Basil Blackwell, 1987   ISBN   0 631 90123 X

A Guide to Student-Centred Learning
Donna Brandes and Paul Ginnis
Basil Blackwell, 1986   ISBN   0 631 14933 3